THE WAY BEYOND THE SHAMAN

Birthing A New Earth Consciousness

THE WAY BEYOND THE SHAMAN

Birthing A New Earth Consciousness

Barry Cottrell

BOOKS

Winchester, UK
Washington, USA

First published by O Books, 2008
O Books is an imprint of John Hunt Publishing Ltd., The Bothy, Deershot Lodge, Park Lane, Ropley, Hants, SO24 0BE, UK
office1@o-books.net
www.o-books.net

Distribution in:

UK and Europe
Orca Book Services
orders@orcabookservices.co.uk
Tel: 01202 665432 Fax: 01202 666219 Int. code (44)

USA and Canada
NBN
custserv@nbnbooks.com
Tel: 1 800 462 6420 Fax: 1 800 338 4550

Australia and New Zealand
Brumby Books
sales@brumbybooks.com.au
Tel: 61 3 9761 5535 Fax: 61 3 9761 7095

Far East (offices in Singapore, Thailand, Hong Kong, Taiwan)
Pansing Distribution Pte Ltd
kemal@pansing.com
Tel: 65 6319 9939 Fax: 65 6462 5761

South Africa
Alternative Books
altbook@peterhyde.co.za
Tel: 021 555 4027 Fax: 021 447 1430

Text copyright Barry Cottrell 2008

Design: Stuart Davies

ISBN: 978 1 84694 121 4

All rights reserved. Except for brief quotations in critical articles or reviews, no part of this book may be reproduced in any manner without prior written permission from the publishers.

The rights of Barry Cottrell as author have been asserted in accordance with the Copyright, Designs and Patents Act 1988.

A CIP catalogue record for this book is available from the British Library.

Barry Cottrell's website
www.earth-awareness.com

Email
barrycottrell@earth-awareness.com

Printed and Bound by Digital Book Print Ltd
www.digitalbookprint.com

O Books operates a distinctive and ethical publishing philosophy in all areas of its business, from its global network of authors to production and worldwide distribution.
This book is produced on FSC certified stock, within ISO14001 standards. The printer plants sufficient trees each year through the Woodland Trust to absorb the level of emitted carbon in its production.

CONTENTS

Preface   vii

Introduction   xi

Part I – An Ice Age Rhapsody   1

1   The Art Of Survival   3
2   The Shaman Of Shanidar   16
3   A Communion Of Consciousness   25

Part II – The Shaman   37

4   Elemental Ecstasy   39
5   Initiation And The Tribe   54
6   Thresholds Between Worlds   65
7   The New Age Shaman   75
8   The Quest For Power   91

Part III – The Spirit Of Shamanism   99

9   At Home On Earth   101
10   Wholehearted Incarnation   108
11   An Agent Of Thought   117
12   Spirit And 'The Spirits'   127
13   Echoes Of Future Grace   136
14   The Vale Of Soul-Making   145
15   Freedom Of Spirit   157

Conclusion   169
Appendixes   175
Notes   182
References   189

For Rosie, with love

PREFACE

The world needs to be 'redeemed' or reclaimed as spirit, and known as possessing soul. For it is soul which embodies spirit, it is spirit which animates soul.

This book was born of the conviction that most of today's critical, global problems, like the wholesale degradation of the planet, have their roots in Western culture's collective denial of the soul and spirit, both in nature and in ourselves. The dominant view of our society is that the natural world is an inanimate resource, there to be exploited for Western consumption. While nature provides the raw materials, human beings are seen as the consumers of products, often made by machines, or else by other human beings forced to behave like machines.

The purpose of this whole exercise is to make profits — to generate economic growth and development. For the denial of soul and spirit in our culture has created a psychic and spiritual vacuum, expressed as an insatiable, collective hunger or greed. In economic terms, this means limitless growth. And it is more than ironic that those who have been pushed to the edge of extinction through Western greed parading as 'development' have been the very tribal peoples worldwide who still see soul in nature, and who have struggled to keep the living flame of Earth's spirit burning in their cultures.

During the last part of the 20th and the beginning of the 21st century, a whole generation of people, loosely termed the 'New Age movement,' have sought to turn back this tide of global devastation by looking for ways to transform themselves, and to reconnect with soul and spirit. Some have been more spiritual, seeking out the airy heights of ancient spiritual disciplines for self-transformation; others have been more soulful, entering into their own pain and woundedness through therapy in the search for healing. Others, still, have sought a more Earth-based and instinctual approach to spirituality in the animistic outlook of tribal peoples and the practices of shamanism.

I count myself as belonging to the last two groups. As a student, I was already 'in search of soul' when I studied academic psychology and philosophy. I didn't find it, and in fact came out of the experience devastated by my encounter with the menacing and deadening spirit of scientific materialism which pervaded both subjects. I then embarked on a long path of inner exploration, for which art was my vehicle of expression, before emerging in the late 1980s with a very definite calling towards shamanism.

There are still many people in tribal societies worldwide, and also some in the West, who have this calling and a need to enact the rituals, practices and role of the traditional shaman in their community. However, this book is called *The Way Beyond The Shaman* as it seeks to move our experience and understanding of shamanism forwards, out of the past, where it has always been centered on the person and practices of the individual shaman. For it is an experience of the *spirit of shamanism* which is going to become more and more essential, and also more accessible, as we enter a new era. Whilst the traditional role and practices of the shaman will remain the specific domain of the gifted few, this book is, in a sense, about the democratizing of shamanism. It presents a vision of shamanism as an experience which is accessible to anyone willing to allow the transformative power and elemental physicality of Earth's spirit into their lives.

In order to move 'beyond the shaman,' this book begins by tracing the roots of shamanism back to the depths of the last ice age, when the special skills of the shaman enabled our Paleolithic ancestors to survive the prolonged crisis of the ice. Part II then examines aspects of shamanic experience, both in traditional, tribal societies, and also in modern, Western culture, where its revival has been taking place in the practices of 'neo-shamanism.'

The actual vision of shamanism presented in Part III of this book comes from my own access to higher frequencies of awareness. As a practicing neo-shaman, I had already begun to bring through 'communications' during my shamanic journeys. Later on I developed this ability to transmit a certain kind of wisdom when in a relaxed, more finely tuned state of consciousness than normal. Call it channeling, call it inspiration, this wisdom arises simply from a willingness to let go and move beyond who we normally think we are into areas of the expanded psyche where we embrace and give voice to the many selves—who we are, who we have been, and who we are becoming—that make up our wider, deeper, and more whole self.

Like the traditional shaman facing their crisis of initiation, we in the West are confronted with the need to transcend the limited idea of who we think we are in order to live more authentic and vital lives. Our survival may well depend upon a radical shift in our understanding of who we are, and in our ability to turn our minds around, so that we once again experience ourselves as part of nature, imbued with soul and spirit. In doing so we may learn to 'see' again with a vision that dissolves the mirage of a dead, mechanical universe, which opens up to the vital essence, to the living presence, that breathes life into the world around us.

INTRODUCTION

A shaman is a man or woman who journeys into unseen worlds of spiritual forces during an altered state of consciousness. The goal of the shaman's passage through these worlds is to obtain help or healing for members of their tribe. The journey is undertaken deliberately, at will, and it is this mastery of awareness—the purposeful navigation of the astral or spirit worlds whilst absent from the physical body—that distinguishes shamanic activity from other psychic work or spiritual disciplines.

Shamanism is the world's most ancient surviving technique for accessing realities beyond the everyday physical world. It was known to the whole of archaic humanity and was being practiced by our Paleolithic ancestors during the last ice age, at least thirty thousand years ago, in the caves of southern France and northern Spain. It is a worldwide tradition, or family of traditions, appearing with remarkable consistency in places as geographically diverse as Siberia, Australia, North America, Central Asia, Malaysia, parts of Africa, and from Central America right down through South America to the tip of Patagonia.

Shamanism is always found in tribal societies living close to nature with little or no technology as we understand the word. It is as if, instead of an industrial technology of artifacts like the car, telephone or computer, the shamans in these cultures have developed the powers of the mind, and of the soul and spirit. In the words of Hopi religious leader, Don Qochvonga, 'I don't blame the white people for their genius to transmit power through their many kinds of machines. They are crude mechanical contraptions that may break down. We Hopis don't need them. We know how to manifest our powers—the same powers—without machines.'[1] The science of native peoples like the Hopi is a highly refined understanding of the unseen spiritual energies which permeate and sustain the natural universe; and their technology is a 'technology of transcendence,'[2] the ability to transcend the usual way of perceiving reality and engage with these subtler forces in the spirit worlds.

Tied to neither time nor place, shamanism appears to be fundamental to the human condition. Many consider it to have been the first spiritual discipline of humankind, the original technique of mystical awakening and the precursor of later spiritual practices. As the most ancient navigator of the human psyche, and beyond, the shaman embodies our innate longing for transcendence—to enter the deepest levels of our being and to drink from the wellspring of consciousness, from the source of life itself.

PART I

AN ICE AGE RHAPSODY

CHAPTER 1

THE ART OF SURVIVAL

As the infant is linked to its mother in a profound participation mystique, even to such a degree that it will absorb, and thus inherit, her tensions and anxieties, so has mankind been linked to the moods and weathers of its mother Earth.
Joseph Campbell, *The Way Of The Animal Powers*[1]

Around 73,500 years ago, an Earth event occurred of such awesome and devastating proportions that it cannot have failed to leave its imprint upon every form of life on the planet, and in particular upon the collective consciousness and memory of the human populations of that time. On the island of Sumatra, a massive volcano called Toba erupted over a period of two weeks, spewing out billions of tons of fine ash and sulphur gases up to twenty-three miles into the atmosphere. No eruption on such an apocalyptic scale is known to have occurred before or since.

What followed was a volcanic winter, with the sun blotted out for years in places, and the rapid spread of ice and snow over large areas of the globe. After six months, most of the volcanic ash had fallen back down to Earth, but by then the sulphur gases had been converting into airborne particles which continued to obscure the sun for years to come. Even when the atmosphere finally cleared decades later, a process had been set in motion of downward spiraling temperatures, the build-up of ice, and ever decreasing sea-levels, as the water from the oceans became land-locked in miles-high glaciers. Within five thousand years temperatures on the surface of the North Atlantic had plunged by up to ten degrees centigrade, sea-levels had dropped by over one hundred and twenty feet, and plants, animals, and people all faced a crisis of survival.

This was not the first time that ice had engulfed almost a third of Earth's surface. Over the last two million years, the planet has been subjected to a good dozen full-blown ice ages. But by the onset of the last ice age, our own early ancestors—'anatomically-modern' humans—had appeared on the prehistoric scene. During the years long, frozen night which followed the eruption of Toba, it was amongst these people that there arose the urgent need for the specialist skills of the shaman.

The impact of the ice

The arrival of the ice and night would have an impact upon the human psyche, the effects of which are still with us today. Our experience of being solitary, isolated individuals is very much a legacy of that time. The trauma of the prolonged darkness, and the remorselessness of pervasive ice, laid down the blueprint, not so much for an evolutionary expansion and unfolding of human consciousness, as for its becoming progressively more tightly bound up within itself.

Deep within the layers of the human psyche there exists a more primal level of awareness, an open innocence that has been superseded by the modern mind. Joseph Campbell has written of this early form of cognition, how 'there became established between the earliest human communities and their landscapes a profound *participation mystique*.' Wherever people went, they encountered plants, animals, hills, all of which 'became their neighbors and instructors, recognized as already there from of old: mysterious presences which in some sacred way were to be known as messengers and friends.'[2] During the warmer interglacial years before the onset of the last ice age our own early ancestors may have experienced a similar kind of spiritual openness and receptive innocence. But with the shock of Toba this state of grace would come to an irreversible end. The prolonged darkness and ice which followed the eruption would mark the onset of a kind of spiritual death, or at least an imprisonment, which would continue right up to the present day.

Before the ice and night set in, the rhythm of the seasons and the abundance of nourishment in the natural world would have been a constant affirmation of Earth's nurturing embrace, as were the winds and the sky. Human consciousness, far from being cut off from Earth's spirit, would have experienced itself within every manifestation of its living, breathing presence. The primal human mind would not have been hidden, located privately inside the brain. Its fluid, expanded awareness would have been more pervasive, extending through the whole physical body, and beyond, into each vibrant natural form it encountered, and out into the very aura and consciousness of Earth itself. But now, with the shock of the ice, came a compression of consciousness, a massive psychic contraction, causing this natural openness, innocence, and fluidity to freeze and shut down. It was as if the collective in-breath of the human psyche got stuck before the out-breath. If you hold your breath long enough, you black out. You lose consciousness. The ancestral mind 'blacked out,' becoming oblivious of its own source, blind to the very ground of its being, and estranged from its own eternal self. With the passing of time, these early ice-age people would no longer be able to tune in instinctively to the unbounded universe of spiritual energies that pervades every aspect of creation. The spiritual realms faded like a forgotten dream, and the energies—or spirits—who live, move and have their being within the natural world, became gods, goddesses, angels, devas, and power animals, once immanent but now transcendent. This would have been the legendary 'fall from grace' of traditional myth and religion. 'The consciousness of man fell in two,' writes Joseph Campbell, 'separated in the awakened mind from the innocence, not only of the beasts without, but also of the beast within, by which the body is shaped, plantlike, in the mother womb....'[3]

As the cold bit deeper, human consciousness would become progressively cut off from Earth's spirit. And within this prolonged absence of warmth lie the origins of shamanism. For it fell to those gifted individuals—the shamans—with a propensity for trance and vision, both to locate the outer meat and also to provide the inner heat for the survival of the Paleolithic tribe. From then on, it would only be these specialist 'technicians of transcendence' who could use their skills to help the tribe retain its link with that former all-embracing awareness, lost during those aeons of seemingly endless time when the sun was banished and the ice held in its grip the very heart of humankind. Through their ability to journey out of the body, the shamans transcended the confines of the ice, bringing back both spiritual warmth and nourishment, and also guidance and information from the worlds of the spirits, needed for the survival of the tribe.

For many other creatures, the challenge of the last ice age was overpowering. At about 15,000 years ago, just when the grip of the ice was beginning to ease off, a wave of extinctions took place, with many species, especially larger mammals, disappearing from the planet; around 11,000 years ago, a further wave of extinctions took away enormous beavers, huge elephants, lions and massive ground sloths, eighteen feet tall. More importantly for our story, the last ice age took with it the only other member of our species, *Homo sapiens*, known to have shared the planet with us modern human beings. Long before the final glaciers had retreated, our human cousins, known as the Neanderthals, had also disappeared.

An epidemic of culture

The Neanderthals occupy what archaeologists call the Middle Paleolithic of prehistory, from at least 200,000 years ago up to their disappearance between 40,000 and 30,000 years ago, at the beginning of the Upper Paleolithic. They lived mainly in Europe and the Levant, spreading as far east as Uzbekistan in western Asia. What these people were like and why they disappeared is one of the great mysteries of the deep past — to be explored in the next chapter. What is clear is that they co-existed in the Middle East with our own early forebears for at least twenty thousand years before the onset of the last ice age, and for another good thirty thousand years after it had started. The earliest traces left by each of these biologically distinct, but neighboring groups are very similar, suggesting that their activities and cultures were alike. That they co-existed peacefully is testified by the enormous timespan during which they shared such a relatively small terrain.

In contrast to the Levant, the Neanderthals in Europe appear to have been on their own for most of that time. This solitary existence came to an end when groups of the 'modern' humans from the Middle East began to migrate westwards, arriving in Europe during the period archeologists call the *Aurignacian,* around 40,000 years ago. Within 10,000 years of this influx, the Neanderthals were extinct. Their disappearance coincides with what has been called an 'epidemic of culture' amongst our Aurignacian ancestors as they moved into Europe. An unparalleled explosion of creativity fired these energetic people, who seem to have been far more like us in the 21st century, than their own Middle East ancestors, fifty thousand years before. As anthropologist Ian Tattershall observes, they brought with them, 'abundant evidence of a fully formed and unprecedented modern sensibility.... Clearly, these people were *us.*'[4]

In culture, outlook and behavior, they were modern. They were intelligent, as we understand the word—bright, creative, ingenious, communicative, enterprising, and quick-witted—and they were probably more skilful with their hands than we are today through practice and use. They invented many new types of stone tool, including tiny flint 'bladelets,' and they converted high quality flint blades into scrapers and burins for engraving. Regional styles of tool sprung up, where before there had only been global uniformity. One use of these tools was to tailor their own clothing—trousers, moccasins, jackets and hats—made, not only from skins and furs for the harsher winter climate, but also from lighter woven materials for the slightly warmer summer months. These they decorated with ornaments—pendants and beads—which were made in great abundance out of mammoth ivory, and also shells, animal teeth, and soft stone. They had a very sophisticated and organized production system for the manufacture of these ornaments. At the site of Abri Castanet, in the Castelmerle valley of southwest France, beads have been found in such vast quantities that it seems likely that they were made for export out of the valley, rather than just for local use.

These were enterprising individuals who liked to travel, both to meet up with other people living in more distant regions, and also to procure materials for their own creative output. For their pendants, beads, and often exquisite carvings, they deliberately chose certain kinds of exotic bone, shell, or ivory, from places far beyond their natural sources in the local neighborhood. The Castelmerle valley itself may have been what Richard Rudgley describes in his book, *Secrets of the Stone Age*, as 'the Aurignacian equivalent of an international trade fair, with peoples from the Atlantic and Mediterranean trading shells and central Europeans bringing mammoth ivory to exchange.'[5]

This was a vigorous and sociable culture, in which physical appearances mattered. The Aurignacians would have had a strong sense of 'self,' as we understand it today, both an inner self-awareness, and an outer social identity. During the thirty thousand years since the eruption of Toba, enough time had passed for the foundations of modern self-consciousness to have been established in these people, overlaying the more primal *participation mystique* of their pre- ice age forebears. That earlier openness would have been rapidly contracting, turning within, and crystallizing down the generations into a new, more alert form of consciousness, with a more focused, well-defined sense of self. Like the tools of the Aurignacians, it would be a self with a sharper, more precise, analytical, cutting edge.

The embryonic stirrings of intellect amongst the earlier 'children of the ice,' as they approached the Upper Paleolithic gave birth to the fully-fledged modern mind of the Aurignacians. It was a mind that — perhaps for the first time — could abstract itself from the here-and-now. It could make plans, and it could *imagine*. But it was also a mind apart, with a separate sense of self — cut off from its source by the remorseless bite of the ice. It had been separated from 'the innocence, not only of the beast without, but also of the beast within...' And out of this separation of their consciousness from its own primal awareness came the unprecedented need amongst these people to reconnect with their own instinctual spirit.

Shamanic cave temples

The Aurignacians may not have been the only or even the first people to exhibit 'a fully formed... modern sensibility.' They were certainly not the only people to be decorating their bodies at that time, for it was already a global, human characteristic. But theirs was a lively and coherent civilization, which flourished under the shadow of the glaciers for a good 14,000 years; and they left behind unique evidence of an irresistible urge to unite and commune with their guardian animal spirits.

Their body ornaments, for example, were worn not simply for display, but to express a certain 'shamanic' sensibility. 'One large class of ornaments,' writes anthropologist Randall White, 'consists of pierced animal teeth, but when teeth were made into pendants, only those of certain species were selected.'[6] From his excavation of the Abri Castanet site in the Dordogne, White has discovered that these people chose to adorn their bodies with the teeth of certain hunting animals, like the fox, the wolf, the hyena, and the bear; and he observes, 'It seems quite likely that the ornament makers of the Aurignacian were, by choosing teeth of certain species, attempting to evoke or assume some of the overall qualities of those species.'[7]

And they didn't just adorn their bodies. They also decorated the walls of the ice-age cave temples uncovered during the 20th century in southern France and northern Spain. Until recently, there were six established giants of Paleolithic cave art, one at Altamira in northern Spain, and the other five in southern France, including the caves of Lascaux—'the Sistine Chapel of the Paleolithic.' All of these caves are thought to have been decorated towards the end of the Upper Paleolithic during the so-called 'Magdalenian' period— between 14,000 and 10,000 years ago. Then, with the discovery in 1991 of the Cosquer caves, submerged off the coast of Marseilles, and in 1994 the monumental Chauvet cave, deep within the limestone gorges of the Archèche, two more ancient giants awoke and re-emerged, bringing to life a formerly impenetrable past, and indicating that shamans were active in this region in the depths of the last ice age during the Aurignacian period, 30,000 years ago.

Prior to the discovery of Chauvet cave, many people viewed the cave paintings and engravings from the Upper Palaeolithic — of which the overwhelming majority are animals — as nothing more than the sympathetic magic of primitive hunting cultures, directed towards success in the hunt. But as archaeologists David Lewis-Williams and Thomas Dowson suggest, 'a significant component of Upper Paleolithic art also derives from altered states of consciousness.'[8] In other words, they are images, not so much of animals hunted in the outside world, but of the 'animal within.' They depict the shamans' power animals, invoked during trance.

Occasional examples of mythical, semi-human figures in other caves, such as the sorcerer of Les Trois-Frères on the edge of the French Pyrenees, had already led bolder commentators like Joseph Campbell to view ice-age cave art as the product of a shamanic culture, in which certain animals are experienced as possessing transcendental qualities in their own right. With the discovery of Chauvet cave, and an abundance of animals hardly renowned for being hunted and eaten as prey, the signs now point very directly towards their being painted for the qualities they possess as power animals. The two animals most frequently depicted in Chauvet are rhinoceroses and lions, dangerous animals that were not on the Paleolithic menu. As guardian spirits they possess strength and courage, essential qualities to assist the shamans in negotiating the rigors of both the visible and the invisible worlds during that harsh epoch.

Shamanism is very much an Earth-centered approach to spirit; and the intimacy of our ice-age ancestors with the substance and spirit of Earth is clear from the very inaccessibility of the cave locations in which they invoked the powers of their animal guardians — described by Joseph Campbell with poetic beauty.

> ...without exception these magical spots occur far from the natural entrances of the grottos, deep within the dark, wandering, chill corridors and vast chambers; so that before reaching them one has to experience the full force of the mystery of the cave itself. Some of the labyrinths are more than

half a mile in depth; all abound in deceptive and blind passages, and dangerous, sudden drops. Their absolute, cosmic dark, their silence, their unmeasured inner reaches, and their timeless remoteness from every concern and requirement of the normal, waking field of human consciousness can be felt even today – when the light of the guide goes out. The senses, suddenly, are wiped out; the millenniums drop away; and the mind is stilled in a recognition of the mystery beyond thought that asks for no comment.[9]

The caves were not inhabited by people; rather, they were visited by shamans to carry out the sacred acts of entering a transcendent reality and bridging the worlds, for the greater well-being of the tribe. While some of the outer cave chambers may have been visited by larger numbers of people, perhaps for communal, ritual functions, the deeper passages and chambers would have been penetrated by the shamans for their more esoterically intimate activities. Reaching the remoteness of these locations would assist them in their transition from a normal to an altered state of consciousness, at the same time as honoring the living body of the 'Great Mother' before they embarked on a shamanic ritual or journey. The deeper they went, the more powerful their experience would be, reflected in the images of more dangerous, and therefore powerful animals, found in the remoter locations.

The shamans would have used sound in order to enter into trance. Evidence from acoustic studies of the locations of cave art suggest that they were chosen partly, or perhaps primarily, for their acoustic properties, acting as natural sound chambers for rhythmical, vocal sounds – and also possibly for drumming – used to carry the shaman across the threshold of consciousness into the spirit worlds.

They would also have used their sense of touch in these dark, interior passages, with the cave wall acting like a permeable membrane between the human psyche and the world of the spirits. The suggestive contours of the cave wall would have indicated to the shaman that their power animal was 'there,' within the wall, waiting to be made manifest through the touch of their fingers as they pressed into the soft clay. By revealing these spirits as images, they would not have been engaging in art as a form of symbolic behavior, with images standing for 'real' animals in the outside world. Rather, the images themselves are 'realistic' — as David Lewis-Williams and Thomas Dowson point out — since they 'depict what people "really" experienced.'[10]

By entering altered states of consciousness, these artist-shamans were able to experience the presence of the spirits, who for most people existed in the worlds beyond. The interior of the caves brought the spiritual dimension so close to the physical that, in the act of painting or engraving, the shamans were simply 'touching and marking *what was already there*.'[11] In making these images, they were externalizing or 'fixing,' the sensed presence of their spirits.

Perhaps this was the first time in human history that a need of this kind had been felt and expressed, to give permanent form to a spiritual reality that had become inaccessible to normal human consciousness. The shamans of the Upper Paleolithic were reaching out to a dimension of life which had formerly been perceived by their ancient ancestors as inherent within the very substance of Earth itself. Through engaging in the rituals of their cave painting and engraving, they were expressing an urgent *religious* need, in the truest sense of religion — to re-connect with Earth's animating spirit which permeates all life.

The art of impermanence

Before the creation of the Upper Paleolithic cave temples, there are few signs of people having had such a pressing, intense need to fix a transcendent reality either in graphic images or in sculptures of bone and stone. Such indelible forms would become a dominant characteristic of future, monumental civilizations, such as Egypt, Greece and Rome. As the human sense of self lost its early openness and fluidity, becoming more crystallized, fixed, and bound by a sense of passing time, so the need grew for long-lasting cultural artifacts which would transcend the limitations of time.

By contrast, the people who lived before the onset of the last ice age have left behind few traces of such a need. Their indigenous sense of being at one with the natural rhythms of life would have given these people a strong awareness of the cycles of growth and decay; and while they almost certainly made art, it would not necessarily have been made to last. Their artistic activities, like the rest of life, would have been subject to the natural forces of creation and destruction.

With the passing of time, and the dislocation of human consciousness from these natural rhythms and cycles, the ice-age psyche would generate rituals to reconnect itself with these forces of nature; and there are signs that some of these later ice-age people actively cultivated an 'art of impermanence,' engaging not only in conscious acts of creation, but also in acts of intentional destruction.

At the major archaeological site at Dolní Vestonice, in Moravia, Czech Republic, evidence has been uncovered that an ice-age people, known as the Pavlovians, had already invented the kiln by 26,000 years ago, and were making their own ceramics. But they were not making pottery as permanent, useful objects. Rather, they made small figurines out of the local loess, or soil, firing them up to such high temperatures that they exploded through 'thermal shock.' This was clearly intentional, since the local loess soil they used was particularly resistant to thermal shock. As the researchers of this site point out, 'Thermal shock did not occur accidentally but required intentional effort and practice.' A figurine would 'shatter with a pop, sometimes sending pieces flying through the air,' and they suggest that 'the whole process could have served some socioritual, perhaps divinational purpose.'[12] While most recent civilizations, going right back to the Egyptians, have been obsessed with art as an act of preservation, the Pavlovians were apparently making art in order to destroy it.

The pyroclastic activities of the Pavlovians in Moravia were taking place relatively close in time to the decoration of Chauvet cave in the French Archèche. These people of around 30,000 years ago were evidently inventive, energetic and passionate, fired by an unprecedented inner need to engage in intense, dynamic rituals, involving both creation and also destruction.

Inner necessity
Between the decoration of Chauvet and of Lascaux a good 15,000 years elapsed—as long a time-span as has passed between the decoration of Lascaux and today. Clearly the Aurignacians had artistic skills that were as fully developed as those of their descendents at Lascaux, some fifteen to twenty thousand years later. Their paintings and engravings possess a continuity of character over this enormous length of time. The cave art of the Upper Paleolithic is easily distinguished from cave art in other parts of the world, and from the art of later civilizations. Something unprecedented happened during this period—something sufficiently persistent to establish a continuity of consciousness between the more recent Magdalenian shamans and their Aurignacian ancestors. What could have sustained this level of awareness?

I believe that it was the remorseless presence of the ice, and that the explosion of creativity, triggering the epidemic of culture, was our ancestors' response to this challenge. For during those 15,000 years, between Chauvet and Lascaux, the deepest bite of the last ice age took place; and just as winter is the most introverted of seasons, so this long winter in the evolution of the human soul and spirit produced a further, deeper rupture between the human psyche and Earth's spirit, a separation which had already begun after the eruption of Toba. Whatever residue the Aurignacians had retained of their early *participation mystique* with the natural expressions of the 'Great Mother' was finally squeezed out of their awareness.

The ice age engendered within these Paleolithic people an urgent need to focus *within*; they developed an inwardness which had not existed before, almost as if they took into themselves the creative forces of nature, which introverted into the now more singular human frame. As the pervasive ice and night bit deeper, our ancestors tapped this well-spring of creativity with a depth of inner penetration that has hardly been surpassed since. Instead of people being part of nature, they now made nature part of themselves, turning it into culture.

Some modern artists—Paul Klee, for example—have talked about creating works of art through 'inner necessity.' The spiritual activities of the Paleolithic shamans were driven by an inner necessity almost beyond comprehension. By crossing the thresholds of awareness and opening up to the inspiration of their transcendent animal allies, they could channel the energies from their spirit helpers' more refined and expanded level of consciousness. They could transcend the ice around them to bring back the riches and inspiration from the spirit worlds for the benefit of their tribe, along with the canny guidance of their power animals. In a world dominated by miles-high glaciers and vast wastelands of frozen tundra, the shamans kept alive the bursting buds of spring, the nurturing warmth of summer, and the fruitful abundance of early autumn, translated into a flowering of human creativity and culture.

This blossoming of the human spirit under the prolonged pressure of the ice would not last. Around 10,000 years ago, at the end of the Upper Paleolithic, the creative fire finally burned down. The ice receded, and human prehistory entered its next phase, known as the Mesolithic Period. The animated restlessness and creative inspiration of our ice-age forebears died down and faded—almost as if the hand of some great Upper Paleolithic *daimon*, which had fired the human spirit during its long trial by ice, withdrew from the drama, its work done. The next chapter in human history would be dull by comparison.

But shamanism was here to stay, not as the religion of future monumental civilizations, but as a technique of tribal survival, wherever humanity lived tight against nature, unprotected by great cities from 'the moods and weathers of its mother Earth.'

CHAPTER 2

THE SHAMAN OF SHANIDAR

The history of our subject, then, is of the progressive enlargement of man's knowledge of the magnitude of his own ignorance and the expansion thereby of his wonder.
Joseph Campbell, *The Way Of The Animal Powers*[1]

The inspired vitality and consummate beauty of such art as has been found in the Chauvet caves suggests that shamanism did not suddenly spring into being 30,000 years ago. Rather its techniques and rituals would have evolved gradually over many millennia, overlapping with the civilization of our Neanderthal cousins before they disappeared some 35,000 years ago; and it is not inconceivable that shamanism is the legacy of a cross-cultural sharing or communion of consciousness between that ancient, earth-rooted branch of the human race and our own early ancestors.

Wholly human beings
Ever since the discovery of the first Neanderthal bones in 1856, near the German town of Düsseldorf, our closest human relatives have been mostly denigrated as sub-human. The stereotyped image of a Neanderthal has been of a creature possessing qualities we like to disown in ourselves — ugly, brutish, barbaric and stupid. Amongst scientists, controversy has raged over whether the Neanderthals were capable of 'symbolic behavior.' Could they think beyond their immediate survival needs, seeing, for example, a human form in the shape of a stone? Could they carve the stone in such a way as to bring out that form? Some scientists think that they lacked the self-awareness and intelligence for this kind of creative activity. Others go even further to suggest that, since they were neither anatomically nor culturally 'modern,' they should not be considered human at all.

Embedded within our culture is the conviction that, as modern human beings, we have a special place in the universe. After all, we not only seem to be the dominant warm-blooded animal on the planet, we are also the only human species here today. We preserve this fragile sense of specialness by raising ourselves above all other forms of life on the planet, past and present, including more ancient human beings like the Neanderthals; and in raising ourselves up, we do all the others down. As James Shreeve, author of *The Neandertal Enigma*, points out, 'For every ounce of human uniqueness we posit in the moderns, we dehumanize the hominid closest to us by precisely that amount.'[2]

In fact the story of human evolution is turning out to be very different from the popular conception of a linear ascent, starting with the most primitive version of the hominid species, culminating in us at the apex of the family tree. Nor has it been a clear-cut path down the ages—one human type at a time—with each new, more slender, upright, and intelligent version replacing its more stooped, ape-like, and dim-witted predecessor. At different times over the aeons of our evolution, there have been many assorted human 'kinds' seeking to co-exist with each other.

Our biological history has been one of repeated evolutionary experiments, of sporadic events rather than a slow, gradual march towards our posture of supremacy today. 'Over the past five million years,' writes anthropologist Ian Tattershall, 'new hominid species have regularly emerged, competed, coexisted, colonized new environments and succeeded—or failed. We have only the dimmest of perceptions of how this dramatic history of innovation and interaction unfolded, but it is already evident that our species, far from being the pinnacle of the hominid evolutionary tree, is simply one more of its many terminal twigs.'[3] Each of these terminal twigs would have had its own form of consciousness, expressed in a variety of cultures—even civilizations. But since archaic human beings have left behind so few tangible artifacts from their early civilizations, most scientists have been forced to conclude that they were somehow less human than we are today.

Science demands hard evidence for its conclusions—evidence

based on observation and measurement. While this is one of its great strengths for understanding the material world, it is also a real limitation when it comes to studying human consciousness, especially prehistoric human consciousness. For what if the need to construct 'permanent' cultural artifacts, like ivory carvings, pottery, or cities of stone, is only a recent development in the human story? What if earlier societies were simply more natural, with no need to make great monumental marks on the environment which leave traces down the ages? Can we only understand what it is to be human by the debris of our past endeavors?

The absence of any tangible signs of creative activity amongst the Neanderthals has led to the view that they lacked the capacity for it, and so were not wholly human. What is more likely is that they were simply not interested in making long-lasting objects. They were probably very sensitive to the natural cycles of growth and decay, and had no inclination to set themselves apart from this natural order. They may have had a more cyclical sense of time recurring, different to our modern sense of time passing. Whether their needs were utilitarian or more symbolic, the means they used to express and satisfy those needs may also have been embedded within the natural processes of growth and decay. Apart from their flint cutting tools, many of which have survived—since they needed to be of hard stone—their other artifacts may have been made out of plant fibres which quickly biodegrade, returning to the earth and leaving no trace.

Neanderthal culture

The fact that Neanderthal people have left so few traces of permanent artifacts does not mean that they never used harder, more durable materials. Recently, a small piece of volcanic stone, found on the Golan Heights in Israel, was dated at 250,000 years old. It shows signs of human intervention, as if an artist had intended to sculpt a female form. If this small stone, known as the 'Berekhat Ram figurine,' is indeed a work of art, then it is 150,000 years older than any other known work of art, and it radically expands the horizon of our scientific understanding of human origins.

While it is hard enough for many scientists to accept that any human being was capable of 'symbolic behaviour' so long ago, what is even more difficult for them to accept is that the Berekhat Ram figurine would have been sculpted by a Neanderthal man, woman, or child, looking out from the Golan Heights across the Mediterranean over a quarter of a million years ago. The dating of the Berekhat Ram figurine has stirred up what was already a hornet's nest of speculation, controversy and prejudice in the academic world.

The traditional view is that art began when *homo sapiens* — anatomically modern men — reached Europe 40,000 years ago after evolving in Africa. They killed off the Neanderthals, decorated themselves with ochre and beads made of animal teeth and painted hundreds of caves with images of deer, mammoth, woolly rhinoceros, fish and other animals and signs.

This eruption of cave painting has long been thought to mark a cultural explosion that occurred when mankind first acquired self-awareness.

If, more than 200,000 years before that, the Neanderthals were capable of "symbolic behaviour," as the creation of artificial human forms is known, the origins of self-consciousness — humanity — lie with them.[4]

What seems certain is that long before we appeared on the prehistoric scene, the people we call 'Neanderthals' were quite capable of carrying out those activities, like making sculptures, which are supposed to characterize modern, human self-consciousness. Perhaps they did not need our more analytical mind in order to be creative. Many artists know from experience that their creativity often requires *a suspension of self-consciousness* before they can allow the more dream-like reality of their mythic imagination to find expression. Often it can only happen once the sharp edge of intellect has dropped away. Perhaps Neanderthal consciousness did lack the sharp edge of intellect, so that their awareness was more permanently steeped within that realm of myth and symbol.

There is absolutely no reason why they would have needed to be self-conscious—in the way that we experience and understand it today—in order to be creative. Nor would they have needed our currently extreme form of self-consciousness to qualify as being human. After all, doesn't real humanity—being truly human—have more to do with love, kindness and compassion, than the ability to be quick-witted, to use language, or to make sculptures?

Neanderthal people may simply have had a sense of self that was different to ours. Far from being dull-minded, they would probably have been highly sensitive to all forms of life in their immediate environment, with which they may have communicated intuitively. Their more expanded awareness would have reduced their need to move around a lot, which is also reflected in the shape of their pelvis. The modern pelvis appears to have been adapted for long-distance walking—a characteristic of our own more restless branch of the human race. Also unlike us, the Neanderthals were probably not very inquisitive or interested in hunting, in the sense of actively planning expeditions to kill animals for food. Rather, they may have been more opportunistic, accepting whatever was provided for them naturally within the bounds of their well trodden, intimately known territories.

Many investigators writing about Neanderthal people have been amazed to discover that they buried their dead 'unlike other animals.' But they were human beings, and their universe would have been permeated with relationship and meaning. Although they appear to have had little need for possessions, they did make objects, like the Berekhat Ram figurine, and they used animal teeth, ivory beads, and bones to display on their bodies. They had a culture, but it did not manifest through a proliferation of artifacts. As prehistorian and archaeologist Paul Bahn points out, 'The Neanderthals were cultured human beings, and we cannot assume that they were incapable of 'modern behaviour.' In fact, we have probably systematically underestimated their technological and symbolic sophistication.'[5]

For years academic debate raged over whether Neanderthals communicated via language. While they may not have had the rapid-fire speech of some modern languages—Spanish, for example—they certainly had the capacity for language. For a long time it was thought that they could only communicate in grunts, lacking the necessary anatomy and intelligence for fluent language. In particular, a bone in the throat, called the 'hyoid,' which helps to produce vowel sounds, was thought to be missing in their anatomy; that is, until a Neanderthal skeleton was discovered in Israel with a hyoid bone just like that of anyone today. They had the use of language, but perhaps *the way* in which they used it was different to ours. Perhaps it was more pictorial, combining words with a sophisticated use of gesture and sound; and rather than a continuous stream of words, using grammar to convey meaning, they might have used words more selectively, on special occasions, uttering them in the true spirit of shamanism, as words or sounds of power.

It is likely that Neanderthal people also engaged in subtle ritual, with a restrained use of symbolic artifacts. At a 50,000 year-old Neanderthal site in southern France the remains of a leopard hide, worn as a costume, were uncovered in 1972. Numerous other sites also indicate that they engaged in ritual, and in particular in a cult of the cave bear—an animal which they appear to have venerated. During the first quarter of the 20th century, three mountain grottoes over 7000 feet high up in the Swiss Alps were excavated—Drachenloch (the Dragon's Den), Wildkirchli (The Wilderness Chapel), and Wildenmannlisloch (the Wild Man's Den). The altitude of these grottoes would have made them inaccessible during the last ice age owing to the incursion of glaciers. The Neanderthal activities which took place within them must have occurred well over 75,000 years ago, before the eruption of Toba. And what was found inside them?

> Charcoal, flints of pre-Mousterian style, flagstone flooring, benches, work tables, and altars for the ritual of the bear—the earliest altars of any kind yet found, or known of, anywhere in the world.
>
> In Drachenloch and Wildermannlisloch little walls of stone,

up to 32 inches high, formed a kind of bin, within which a number of cave-bear skulls had been carefully arranged. Some of these skulls had little stones arranged around them; others were set on slabs; one, very carefully placed, had the long bones of a cave bear (no doubt its own) placed beneath its snout; another had the long bones pushed through the orbits of its eyes.[6]

Joseph Campbell suggests that this bear's bones were pushed through its eye-holes to 'avert the danger of the evil eye,' after the bear had been sacrificially killed. In these most ancient of tabernacles — with the careful attention paid to the placing of the skulls, and to the arrangement of the bones and stones — we have evidence of subtle and sophisticated ritual. They are activities which testify — as Joseph Campbell so eloquently points out — 'to the force of the mythic imagination in the ordering of life in Neanderthal times...'[7]

A caring community
That Neanderthal people also engaged in an early form of shamanic activity — implying healing and caring within a community — is backed up by a major discovery in the late 1950s of a cave in Iraq's Zagros Mountains, where the remains of nine Neanderthal people were found. Located at Shanidar, 250 miles north of Baghdad, this enormous cave is 132 feet deep with a mouth 175 feet wide. It contains several levels of remains, representing about 100,000 years of human existence.

One of the people buried there around 40,000 years ago had been seriously injured during his life, sustaining terrible wounds to his head and body. An arm had withered and he was blind in one eye. He could only have survived by relying on others. He was clearly a member of a caring, compassionate community which looked after its weaker fellows, rather than of a troop of insensitive brutes, surviving according to the harsh dictates of survival of the fittest.

The most significant find in this cave, however, was a male skeleton of about 5 foot 8 inches — tall for a Neanderthal — with a badly crushed skull. This man had lived around 60,000 years ago and may have died when the roof of a cave he was in collapsed. His body had been laid on a bed of evergreen boughs which was heaped with flowers. Microscopic analysis of the surviving pollens has identified eight species or more, mainly related to the grape hyacinth, bachelor's button, hollyhock and yellow-flowering groundsel. Seven of the eight species are used today in Iraq as medicinal herbs.

The excavator of this cave, Ralph Soleki of Columbia University, was sure that these flower pollens had not been introduced accidentally to the cave and that they had been laid down purposely with this now famous 'Shanidar IV' burial. 'The hollyhock is especially indicative of this,' writes Soleki, 'since it grows in separate individual stands, and cannot be grasped in bunches like the others. Some person or persons once ranged the mountainside, collecting these flowers one by one.'[8] The plants were clearly selected deliberately for their medicinal and also, probably, for their symbolic properties. Soleki goes on to make the most telling of observations.

> It may be simply coincidence that the flowers found with Shanidar IV have medicinal or economic value (at least in our present knowledge), but the coincidence does raise speculation about the extent of human spirit in Neanderthals.
> One may speculate that Shanidar IV was not only a very important man, a leader, but also may have been a kind of medicine man or shaman in his group.[9]

Neanderthal people were caring and intimate, not only with each other but also with the natural world around them. They may have had their own forms and uses of language, reflecting their own quality of self-consciousness, which was probably quite different to ours. Joseph Campbell suggests that our experience today of being separate, self-conscious individuals is 'of a secondary order, a mere effect of the way in which lightworld consciousness experiences objects within a conditioning frame of time and space. More deeply, more truly, we are of one life...'[10] We may speculate that Neanderthal people were still aware of this fundamental, unifying ground of all life, and that their consciousness had not—and could not—split in two, as did ours, with intellect eclipsing instinct and intuition. If they had retained the pre-verbal 'animal innocence' of the primal mind, this would have given them a dominant sixth sense—a naturally extended form of perception—reflected in the shape of their heads, with the prominent brow and nose.

Their conscious life may have been more like a meditation, a *participation mystique* with Earth's spirit, which became lost to our own ancestors, and to future generations. Their shamans may not have needed to journey out of the body to engage with the world of spirit, because they would have been able perceive and interact with it directly, as, perhaps, could all Neanderthals. The special qualities which made a person a shaman might have been a gift for healing and perhaps also a certain numinous power through which he or she became the focus or center of the tribe.

While our understanding of Neanderthal consciousness is bound to be largely conjecture, there are certain telling signs suggesting that they possessed a form of spiritual awareness, which would have provided the basis for later shamanic practices, as we understand them today. And it is possible that shamanism evolved through a communion of spirits between these more ancient human cousins of ours, and our own ice age ancestors.

CHAPTER 3

A COMMUNION OF CONSCIOUSNESS

'Ronnie,' Grof continued, 'you mentioned before that until there were the appropriate tools, the inner visions could not be correlated with external, scientific facts. Would you agree that now we have these tools, somehow we should be able to combine information that comes from these inner states with knowledge gained through objective science and technology into a totally new vision of reality?'

'That's right, Laing agreed. 'I think...that conjunction is the most exciting adventure of the contemporary mind.'[1]

Stanislav Grof and R.D. Laing, in Fritjof Capra, *Uncommon Wisdom*

The anatomy of self-consciousness

As far as physique was concerned, Neanderthal people do seem to have conformed to the popular stereotype of a muscle-bound hunk. They were immensely muscular and strong. But that is as far as the popular conception goes. For the other aspect of that stereotype — of Neanderthal dim-wittedness — has absolutely no foundation. Their brains were actually slightly larger than ours, and, as James Shreeve observes, they must have used them for something."....a big brain is an expensive piece of adaptive equipment. You don't evolve one if you don't use it. Combining enormous physical strength with manifest intelligence, the Neandertals appear to have been outfitted to face any obstacle the environment could put in their path. They could not lose."[2]

As we shall see, it was *because of* their unique kind of intelligence, and *because of* their high degree of sensitivity, reflected in their big brain, that they did eventually 'lose' (although it was perhaps more a case of their *withdrawing* from life on Earth than of their 'losing'). In any event, they disappeared during the latter half of the last ice age; and in order to understand why they disappeared, we need to look more closely at what made them different to us. Somehow, the way in which they encountered life on Earth made it impossible for them to stay here.

They had differently shaped heads to ours, especially their faces, with heavy brow-ridges, big noses and protruding midfacial regions. Cranial features like these do suggest that Neanderthal consciousness was different to ours and to that of our ancestors. What does science say about these differences?

Humans are.... unique among mammals in lacking facial projection: the face of the adult *Homo sapiens* lies almost entirely beneath the anterior cranial fossa, whereas the face in all other adult mammals, including Neanderthals, projects to some extent in front of the braincase.[3]

Anatomically, many of the cranial features which make us uniquely modern and human in appearance—like a globular braincase, a vertical forehead, a small browridge and pronounced chin—all stem from the central bone in the base of the skull, called the 'sphenoid,' failing to develop fully. This phenomenon of 'sphenoid reduction' means that the face does not project forwards, as it does with all other mammals including Neanderthal people. It may be an example of what evolutionary scientists call 'paedomorphosis' or regressive evolution. An organism adapts or evolves by *withholding* a process of growth, which would normally lead to fully developed adult features. It retains into adulthood the features of an earlier stage of development, like childhood. From this perspective, our modern appearance, and consciousness, could be seen as a regressive adaptation from the normal line of hominid development, to which we belong. Something happened in our evolution to set us apart from our ancient hominid ancestry.

In the first chapter, it was suggested that modern humans survived the impact of the last ice age through a form of psychic introversion—a contraction or crystallization of consciousness.

This constriction of the psyche gave birth to our modern form of intelligence, but it also cut us off from our instinctual spirit, and from our more animal or elemental sense of belonging to life on Earth. Could this contraction of consciousness be reflected in our uniquely regressive anatomy of the brain, in our sphenoid reduction, which is absent in the Neanderthals? And could this be the key to our having survived the ice age and to the disappearance of the Neanderthals?

While science can show us the physical anatomy of our evolution, it generally refuses to speculate about consciousness, or the psychospiritual aspects of our development. We need to seek alternative sources—knowledge from 'inner visions' and 'inner states'—to complement the discoveries of science. In order to penetrate the mystery of Neanderthal humanity and consciousness, I sought further information and understanding from a reliable channeled perspective, and asked Gildas, Ruth White's discarnate wise guide, to comment.

Alter major awareness

> Neanderthal man had enormous access to the alter major chakra. The different shaping of the head showed the size and function and awareness and necessity of the alter major chakra.[4]

The 'alta' major chakra was mentioned in the writings of the esotericist Alice Bailey. In Ruth White's own book, *Working With Your Chakras*, she describes how this chakra, located in the head near the bottom of the skull, is very much connected to instinct and to the old cortex or 'lizard brain.' An awakened alter major chakra, she says, 'puts us in touch with the non-verbal message system which protects us from danger.'[5] It is that instinct which tells animals to flee from a terrain just before an earthquake or some other natural disaster, a sixth sense which we have lost. And she points out, 'If this sense had not been so universally lost or dishonored, our planet might not now be facing imminent disaster.'[6]

The alter major chakra is also the chakra which opens up morphic resonance and awareness of what has gone on in our history, of whatever has been the experience of any part of the human race in the past. Gildas has pointed out that since the energies of this chakra have been shut down during the course of our evolution, we now suffer a kind of amnesia about important, formative experiences in our collective past. It seems that Neanderthal people had a very deep sense of the living past, of the succession of generations, and that they were able to draw upon this ancestral knowledge and experience in the same way that we today, perhaps, 'surf the internet' for information. They had greater access to the collective unconscious and their larger brain capacity reflects this ability to draw on and integrate experience from a wider, deeper space-time continuum than we are used to now.

Finally Ruth White points to the devic nature of the alter major chakra which 'strengthens our contact with plants, trees, animals, rocks, elements, seasons, growth cycles and the substance of earth itself.'[7] An awakened alter major chakra links us with Earth's spirit, and with the Pan-inspired energies which make us, literally, more *vitally* aware of life, both within and around us. When we lose our awareness of Earth's natural rhythms and cycles, when we shut down or contract our consciousness away from the natural world, 'we foster duality and increase our vulnerability to deep levels of sickness which are resistant to healing.'[8]

It was because of their sensitivity to the natural world, and their direct, subtle interactions with the spirits of nature, that Neanderthal people 'constructed' a civilization that would be virtually invisible to later generations. The focus of their awareness was totally different to ours. But, as Gildas points out, their civilization would have still been a profoundly organized affair.

> If you take the more natural point of view — that of the extreme organization that there is in the natural rhythms and cycles — then it will be seen that Neanderthal man was a highly

organized civilization, but in a totally more natural way, an intuitive, instinctual and pre-verbal way.[9]

An opened alter major chakra is a quality which our Neanderthal cousins shared with all other mammals. It gave them their instinctual awareness and the experience of belonging to the natural world.

The gift of Neanderthal man to humanity has really been the development of the alter major chakra, although it got closed down. But now it is being opened up, so that there will be a gradual movement and recognition that everything that a human being needs doesn't necessarily have to be learned through the intellect — that it is imprinted at a different level from the DNA at a sort of subtle echo of the DNA; and Neanderthal man gives a lot of that gift to humanity.[10]

Significantly, the physical location of this chakra is the region around the *sphenoid bone* at the base of the skull. Could 'sphenoid reduction' be science's way of describing physically and anatomically an inactive alter major chakra?

With a deeper understanding of who Neanderthal people were, and why they disappeared, we can no longer deny them their humanity. Rather, we may seek to restore what was lost when they withdrew from life on Earth, and to become ourselves more 'wholly human.' For as Gildas points out, their gift to us today — as we shift towards a new consciousness — is this very ability to apprehend life more holistically, instinctively and intuitively, no longer dominated by the narrow focus of the modern mind. Theirs was a whole 'other' way of being, of perceiving and understanding the world, which was lost to humanity, but which may now be regained.

The primal mind
The Neanderthals seem to have possessed a natural, instinctive spirituality. That their consciousness was a form of expanded

awareness, characteristic of the primal mind, is also supported by James Shreeve in his epic of scientific journalism, *The Neandertal Enigma*, which surveys the most important scientific research carried out in the 20th century into the mystery of the Neanderthals — who they were, how they might have been related to us 'moderns,' and why they died out. His conclusion about Neanderthal consciousness, based upon his extensive research, provides a further, intuitive insight into their legacy to us today.

> The purpose of knowledge, to a Neandertal, would not be to gain control, but to increase intimacy, not just between individuals but between the individual mind and whatever it sees, touches, smells, and remembers.
>
> To this end, I imagine Neandertals possessing a different sort of self and a different kind of consciousness..... The borders between the Neandertal and the Neandertal world are fuzzy. For us, consciousness seems like an inner "I" resting somewhere deep in the mind, eavesdropping on our stream of thoughts and perceptions. This, of course, is a neuro-fiction; there is no special centre of the brain where consciousness resides. I would give the Neandertals a fictive inner voice, too, but move it out, away from the centre, so that it speaks from nearer to that fuzzy border with the world.[11]

The Neanderthal mind would have had a fluid and holistic perception of the natural universe to which it knew it belonged. It would have been 'intimate' in the true sense of the word, possessing a profound knowledge of the natural world through being deeply embedded *within* it. These people may have lived primarily in the eternal 'now,' with gentle, permeable boundaries between 'self' and 'other.'

> A Neandertal thought would be much harder to abstract from the thing or circumstance that the thought is about. The perception of a tree in a Neandertal feels like the tree; grief over a lost companion is the absence and the loss. Neandertal psyche

floats on the moment, where the metaphor of consciousness as a moving stream is perfect, the motion serene and unimpeded by countercurrents of re-think, counter-think, and doublethink. I picture two Neandertals sitting side-by-side, their intimacy so exact that their interior voices cross and coalesce, like two streams merging into a river, their waters indistinguishable.[12]

Shreeve is portraying here the primal mind, our ancient mystic participation with Earth's spirit and with each other. It was a mind open to the flow of Earth's organic current of awareness running through and between every manifestation of creation. The Neanderthals were not driven to be creative, as we understand the word, or to build an extensive culture of artifacts, since, for them, the rhythms, cycles and expressions of the natural world were their creativity and culture. Nor does the relative absence of ritual artifacts in their culture mean that they lacked a religious sensitivity or spiritual awareness.

I think the Neandertals had natural spirits like those of modern peoples who also live tight against nature. But where the modern's gods might inhabit the eland, the buffalo, or the blade of grass, the Neandertal's spirit *was* the animal or the grass blade, the thing and its soul perceived as a single vital force, with no need to distinguish them with separate names. Similarly, the absence of artistic expression does not preclude the apprehension of what is artful about the world. Neandertals did not paint their caves with the images of animals. But perhaps they had no need to distil life into representations, because its essences were already revealed to their senses. The sight of a running herd was enough to inspire a surging sense of beauty. They had no drums or bone flutes, but they could listen to the booming rhythms of the wind, the earth, and each other's heartbeats, and be transported.[13]

For Neanderthal people, their symbolic acts were perhaps more simple, more natural, and less obvious as rituals than the more elaborate, complex rituals of future civilizations. For example, placing the skull of a cave bear on a rock in a cave, so that it could be used to invoke the collective energies or spirit of this venerated animal, is a form of ritual. But given their ability to identify naturally with both the inner presence and the outer expression of the living universe anyway, seeing no difference between the two, they may have had little need for ritual objects designed to promote this state of *participation mystique*. The need for ritual artifacts or totem objects in itself belies a certain loss of connection with the spirits whom the artifacts are helping to invoke.

While this natural openness to the universe was the Neanderthal gift to our ancestors in the Palaeolithic world, it was also their vulnerability, and may have been, ultimately, the reason behind their disappearance.

The legacy of the ice

After the eruption of Toba, the long frozen night of the most recent ice cycle really set in. For the Neanderthal population this proved in the long run to be a challenge which they could not face. With their extended awareness and natural ability to identify with the conditions around them, their spirits would have frozen and died. Instead they moved on, withdrawing eventually from life of Earth.

Our modern ancestors, by contrast, would have already been developing the intellectual ability to abstract and dissociate themselves from their circumstances, and to experience the creative forces of nature as a cultural drive within. With the challenge of the ice came the challenge to the spirit. The human heart began, in a sense, to freeze, and the mind to crystallize. Unlike their Neanderthal cousins, our Palaeolithic ancestors adapted to the ice by contracting their consciousness. It is as if they adapted by 'hardening' or 'freezing' consciousness in a way that the Neanderthals could not. As their consciousness contracted and crystallized, becoming progressively abstracted from the natural ebb and flow of life, intellect began to replace instinct and intuition as the primary mode of cognition, as the means of perceiving and knowing the world. Instead of telepathic communication — common amongst Neanderthal people — our ice age ancestors would have come more and more to rely on external channels of communication, as we do today, through which to express their explosion of culture.

Neanderthal people did not need culture of this kind. Nor could they abstract themselves from the natural world in which they were embedded and to which they belonged. For that *was* their culture. They did not need to create a culture of monuments and artifacts in order to express the essence of life within and around them. Their greatest need was for the warmth of intimacy that comes from a shared sense of belonging to Earth and to each other; and so it remained.

But this need was becoming both more and more threatened by Earth's trial by ice, and also incompatible with the direction in which our Palaeolithic ancestors' development was going. Neanderthal people were profoundly conservative, and they were becoming confused by our ancestors' curiosity and ingenuity. They were also disturbed by their younger human cousins' emerging need for control over nature, and by their growing sense of separation. For whatever traces of alter major awareness our ancestors may have had, began to shut down completely, as their instincts were replaced by the first glimmerings of cool intellect. In that sense, they were succumbing to the penetrating chill of Earth's trial by ice. They had become self-conscious, in the sense of apprehending life through the narrow, crystallized self. In that contraction of self, they began to experience themselves more and more as separate individuals, and less as belonging to the greater whole.

James Shreeve suggests that, 'If human evolution were an epic, the Upper Palaeolithic would be the chapter where the hero comes of age.'[14] People were, for the first time, becoming self-aware, in that more modern, sharp-edged, well-defined sense of 'self.' And while, today, a solid, grounded sense of self is an essential vehicle for negotiating the rigors of modern life, the cost of self-consciousness has been our expanded awareness and intimacy with the natural world. This was the original gift of our Neanderthal cousins to our ancestral shamans, for without their contact with the Neanderthals, our Palaeolithic ancestors may well have lost touch with the worlds of spirit altogether. But through a communion of spirits, the Neanderthal shamans would have shared their spiritual vision with the psychically gifted individuals amongst our forebears. That this sharing of spiritual vision did take place is suggested by a significant find deep within the 30,000 year-old Chauvet cave, decorated by our Aurignacian shaman ancestors. The seasoned cavers who discovered the cave describe the scene within Skull Chamber.

> In the middle of the chamber, on a block of grey stone of regular shape that had fallen from the ceiling, the skull of a bear was placed as if on an altar. The animal's fangs projected beyond it into the air. On the top of the stone there were still pieces of charcoal, the remains of a fire-place. All around, on the floor, there were more than thirty bear skulls; now covered in a frosting of amber-covered calcite, they were purposely set out on the earth. There were no traces of skeletons. This intentional arrangement troubled us because of its solemn peculiarity.[15]

Over the fifty to sixty millennia during which the more ancient Neanderthals had cohabited with their younger cousins, our ancestors, there was clearly a deep sharing, not only of their spiritual awareness and understanding, but also of the mystic relationship which existed between them and the cave bear. While members of these two groups may or may not have interbred physically, the Neanderthals would have communicated their own direct experience of at-one-ness with the natural universe to our Palaeolithic ancestors, perhaps helping them to maintain their capacity for expanded awareness despite the crisis of the ice. But with the passing of time, and with the disappearance of the Neanderthals, these ice-age shamans would find themselves more and more only able to enter into this state of mystical consciousness by leaving the physical body, and by journeying to the worlds of spirit. For whatever ability they may once have had to perceive spirit and act upon it directly was being lost, as their normal state of consciousness became too bounded by the ice.

For the Neanderthals, their contact with our Palaeolithic forebears generated an intolerable psychic pressure—to adapt by contracting their more diffuse, expanded selves. But they could not do this. Instead, they withdrew from a world where fear and ice had cut across the natural rhythms and cycles of their life, and where, as Gildas points out, the sharp edge of intellect was clearly becoming the dominant tool for human survival.

> Neanderthal man disappeared because intellect was put above instinct and there was no ground for marrying the two. They disappeared because they could no longer compete, and because their identity became in doubt, was suspect. But the Earth holds their pattern and the Earth now is putting forward a very strong voice for that pattern to be re-recognised.[16]

Despite their disappearance, Earth still 'holds their pattern.' The indigenous Neanderthal spirit survived, not so much in the techniques of shamanism for journeying out of the body, as in the living energy, or spirit of shamanism. This is the pattern which Earth holds—our ability to perceive directly nature's mythic and spiritual dimension. It is this spirit of shamanism which Earth is calling so strongly for us to recognize again today.

PART II

THE SHAMAN

CHAPTER 4

ELEMENTAL ECSTASY

The pre-eminently shamanic technique is the passage from one cosmic region to another – from earth to sky or from earth to the underworld. The shaman knows the mystery of the break-through in plane.
Mircea Eliade, *Shamanism: archaic techniques of ecstasy*[1]

The word shaman comes from the Tungus tribe of Siberia and means *one who sees in the dark* or *one who knows*. Shamanic peoples believe in the existence of other worlds which permeate or interpenetrate our own ordinary everyday reality. To the average person these worlds are invisible or 'dark,' populated by spiritual forces and beings that cannot be perceived by our normal senses. The shaman, however, is someone who has opened the inner eye, who can 'see.' Joe Green, a Paviotso Indian from Pyramid Lake, Nevada, describes this darkness which only the shaman can know or see.

> There are two nights. The second one comes behind the night that everybody sees. This second night is under the darkness. It tells the shaman where the pain is and what caused the sickness. When the second night comes it makes the shaman feel that he is a doctor. The power is in him to doctor. Only shamans can see this second night. The people can see only the darkness. They cannot see the night under it.[2]

The shaman's power to see and handle forces which are invisible to normal waking consciousness is often acquired through a spiritual crisis, an initiatory experience of suffering through which the shaman-to-be undergoes a seismic shift in their orientation towards life – an 'inward relocation of the real at the expense of...everyday consciousness.'[3] It is an experience of psychic or spiritual death and rebirth, an entry into darkness where the shaman undergoes a transformation of consciousness, a renewal of self, imbued with the numinous power of the preconscious or primal mind.

Mystical heat

One possible root of the word *shaman* is the Sanskrit term *sram* meaning 'to heat oneself or practice austerities.'[4] Shamanic initiation, like many Eastern and Western spiritual practices, may be seen as a process of self-purification, a path requiring dedication, solitude and, at times, abstinence or 'the practice of austerities.' At the same time, it also implies mastering an inner fire which generates heat and light within and eventually bestows the power to 'see.' While the lighting and kindling of this inner fire is generally accomplished through pain, psychic dislocation and turbulence, the shaman emerges from the experience transformed, not so much the 'wounded healer' but, as Joan Halifax observes, the 'healed healer': 'Those who have gone through this initiatory crisis are often more gifted, heartier, more full of humor, and wiser than most individuals in his or her culture.'[5]

Harnessing the combustive energies experienced during initiation allows the shaman to develop an inner luminosity — what Australian Aborigines call 'the strong eye' — from which they acquire shamanic sight and knowledge of invisible worlds. This mystical heat creates a kind of psychic transparency in the shaman, rendering the normally opaque veil between the worlds equally transparent. During his trek across the Arctic from Greenland to Alaska during the early 1920's, Knud Rasmussen was told about this inner illumination by an Iglulik shaman. It consists of

> a mysterious light which the shaman suddenly feels in his body, inside his head, within the brain, an inexplicable searchlight, a luminous fire, which enables him to see in the dark, both literally and metaphorically speaking, for he can now, even with closed eyes, see through darkness and perceive things and coming events which are hidden from others; thus they look into the future and into the secrets of others.[6]

The first time this mystical luminous fire is experienced by the shaman

> it is as if the house in which he is suddenly rises; he sees far ahead of him, through mountains, exactly as if the earth were one great plain, and his eyes could reach to the end of the earth. Nothing is hidden from him any longer; not only can he see things far, far away, but he can also discover souls, stolen souls, which are either kept concealed in far strange lands or have been taken up or down to the Land of the Dead.[7]

Amongst the Bushmen of the Kalihari, the words they use for *shaman* emphasize the supernatural potency of this fiery, illuminatory process. For example, the northern Bushman words are *n/um k'ausi*, meaning 'owner or master of potency.' N/um is the mysterious vital force or potency being tapped by the Bushman shamans during their trance dancing. It is experienced as increasing heat while they go into trance. Lorna Marshall, who lived with the northern Bushmen and studied their healing practices, looks upon this potency rather like electricity, an undifferentiated, impersonal force, which is always strong and, when harnessed, can be useful. When uncontrolled, it can become too intense and dangerous. The Bushmen call *n/um* a 'death thing' and also a 'fight,' expressions which they use for anything strong or dangerous, such as certain animals, or the sun.[8]

Bushman shamans use the rhythm of the breath and hyperventilation to bring their *n/um* or potency to the boil as they enter trance. The exertions of their seeming tireless dancing heats the *n/um* which is experienced physically as a substance in the pit of the stomach. Along with the women's singing, which the men say 'awakens their hearts,' their dancing eventually brings their *n/um* to the boil. At this point the stomach muscles become knotted in contractions that force the dancers' bodies forward into a bent position. Sometimes their noses bleed. The *n/um* becomes so hot that it turns to steam, bubbling up the spinal column. According to the Bushman shaman, Kau Dwa, 'In your backbone you feel a pointed something and it works its way up. The base of your spine is tingling, tingling, tingling.'[9] On arriving in the head, the *n/um* moves to the crown where it gives rise to the experience of *!kia*, 'shamanic' enlightenment, and the ability to see and cure the causes of illness in others. The trance healer has X-ray vision and can see over great distances. As one Bushman master of *n/um* expressed it: 'When I make the *n/um* rise, it explodes and tosses me into the air; I enter heaven and finally fall back down again.'[10] It is only once the force of *n/um* has been brought under control that it can be used for healing: 'Its heat is simultaneously activated and held in check, not only by the dancer himself, but also communally, through the ritualized dancing and songs of the group, where the control, as well as the excitation, is governed by the clapping, singing, and pacing of the whole affair by the women.'[11] If the *n/um* boils up too quickly, the women offer men water with which to cool off; they also watch to protect them so that they don't fall into the camp fires during trance.

The nocturnal trance dance is central to Bushman healing practices, taking place perhaps four times a month, with each dance reaching its first climax around midnight. It may sometimes continue for a day and a half with a second peak at the following sunrise. Amongst the Bushmen the association with fire and going into trance is a predominantly male attribute since they believe that trances can harm babies being carried by women during both present and future pregnancies. The time when women too enter trance is during a special women's dance, usually after menopause has started. Under normal circumstances it is small groups of men who dance to the sharp rhythms of the women's clapping and chanting; and although the roles of men and women in Bushman society are very distinct and their activities generally kept apart, Lorna Marshall observes that 'The curing dance draws people of a Bushman band together into concerted action as nothing else does. They stamp and clap and sing with such precision that they become like an organic being. In this close configuration — together — they face the gods.'[12]

Many observers have remarked how closely the Bushman

shaman's description of the rising *n/um* resembles the raising of the *kundalini* energy in Eastern spiritual practices. Tibetan yogis, for example, are well-known for their ability to control their body heat, withstanding long exposure to low temperatures whilst wrapped only in sheets dipped in icy water. English-born Lama and Tantric shaman, Ngakpa Chögyam Rinpoche explains this yoga of mystical heat—*tu-mo*—practiced by a particular kind of yogi called a *repa*.

Well, the term *yogi* (*naljorpa* in Tibetan) means "one who rests in the natural state"—that is, someone who has profound realization and yogic powers, such as the facility for lucid dreaming, or the ability to radically increase body temperature through the practice of *tu-mo*, the yoga of mystical heat.....

The word *repa* means "cotton-wearer," because repas vow to wear only cotton clothing, no matter how cold the weather gets. The main point of tu-mo practice is to "stare into" the sensation of inner fire and realize its empty nature as the primal purity of all things. In the past, the tu-mo power of some repas was such that they used to live above the snow line and wear nothing at all because of the inner fire they'd developed.[13]

Whilst harnessing this mystical heat—and obtaining the inner illumination which enables one to 'see'—may be an essential step on the path towards becoming a shaman, it is clearly a quality also found amongst mystics, seers, holy men and medicine women all over the world at all times; and although the Bushmen's *!kia* may not be identical to the *samadhi* of the Eastern mystic, the processes of 'inner combustion' leading to each respective state of vision or enlightenment equally appear to be very similar. For example, James Cowan has described how young Australian Aborigines go through an initiation to become a *karadji*, or 'clever man'—the Aboriginal shaman. A potential clever man is already distinguished from other people by 'the light radiating from his eyes,'[14] but an important part of their initiation involves spirits inserting crystals into their bodies, and it is this crystallized light which bestows upon them their power, or *miwi*. Like the Bushman's *n/um*, the Aboriginal shaman's *miwi* enables him to 'see,' to 'seize what is imperceptible,' and 'bridge the gap between what is manifested and the spirit-world of the Dreaming.'[15] Also like the Bushman's *n/um*, Australian shamans locate their *miwi* in the pit of the stomach and use breathing techniques to induce their visionary experiences. Again, the similarity to the raising of the *kundalini* 'serpent power' in Eastern spiritual traditions is striking, all the more so in the case of the Australian shamans since snakes play an important part in their initiation ceremonies and are closely associated with the power of quartz crystals to open the inner eye.

What is evident here is that shamans, psychics and seers — as well as many mystics, medicine men and women — all share a special relationship with the inner heat or luminous fire that enables them to 'see.' Like the ability to sing, seeing is latent in all human beings, although it is only developed by these specialists, who tend to be more naturally gifted than others. Even though the word *shaman* may mean 'one who knows, or one who sees in the dark,' this ability to see or know on its own is not sufficient to distinguish the experiences of the shaman from those of the psychic or mystic. To do this, we need to examine the nature of the shaman's ecstatic flight into the world of the spirits.

Magical flight

The practices of the shaman have been immortalized in the title of Mircea Eliade's classic text, *Shamanism: Archaic techniques of ecstasy*.[16] While ecstasy is normally thought of as an experience of spiritual exaltation, rapture or bliss, when applied to shamanism it refers specifically to the altered state of consciousness which the shaman enters in order to cross over the threshold between worlds and to journey through the metaphysical domain. In fact, the Greek term *ekstasis* means just that, 'experiencing the action of moving through space,' and navigating the inner worlds is precisely what a shaman does that is different to a medium, a psychic, a spiritual healer, or a person channeling.

With their natural propensity for trance, many shamans may

also be mediums. But the experiences which the shaman and the medium undergo during their altered state of consciousness are entirely different. The simple distinction is that mediums, channels, and spiritual healers carry out their work by allowing the spirits to come *to* them. They tend to work in a vertical position, seated or standing up. This means that a significant proportion of their overall energy remains centered within the physical body, allowing it to be an effective channel for the spirits or healing energies. Only their self-consciousness, located around the upper part of the body—the head and shoulders—is relaxed, suspended, or slightly displaced.

Shamans, by contrast, nearly always journey on the ground, either seated or lying down. This allows them to leave the body more or less completely and to go *to* the spirits, meeting them, as it were, in their own terrain. While the trance medium will remember little, if anything, of their experience, the shaman is generally conscious whilst out of the body. He or she remains very alert throughout the journey and will remember most of its details after returning to ordinary consciousness. Shamans have been called 'masters of spirits,' emphasizing this active rather than passive relationship with the spirit worlds. By completely disengaging their consciousness from the body, the dynamic energies of the will are freed up for action—for their magical flight through the dramatic and sometimes dangerous astral worlds of the spirits.

The purpose of the shaman's journey is directly linked to the shamanic understanding of sickness, in which people generally become ill because of soul-loss. Their souls may have been stolen by 'sickness spirits' and taken to the spirit worlds; or something fearful, like a shock or an accident, may have driven a person's soul out of their body. The soul then gets stuck, lost or held in the spirit worlds. The task of the shaman, and one of the main purposes of shamanic flight, is to navigate through these worlds in search of the displaced soul. Having tracked it down to the place where it is lost or hidden, the shaman then brings it back to its owner.

The vehicle for this magical flight is usually monotonous

drumming, although in some cultures other means—like the singing and clapping of the Bushman women, and the hyperventilation of the trance dancers—are used to induce an altered state of consciousness. Especially important in Central and South America is the use of magical plants to release the soul from the body for the shamanic journey. For example, the Huichols of Mexico ingest *hikuri*, the hallucinogenic cactus peyote, while the Tukanoan peoples of the northwest Amazon drink the bitter *ayahuasca*, the 'vine of the soul,' in order to confer with the spirits of the forest. The Yanomami of the Venezuelan Amazon inhale *ebena*, the 'semen of the sun,' which completely dissolves the shaman's experience of ordinary reality.

Despite this wide use of hallucinatory drugs by South American shamans, riding the sound of the drum is the most universal, and possibly the most archaic method used by shamans for entering other realities. The use of sound has always been central to the rituals and ceremonies of tribal peoples. But the drum is distinguished from all the other instruments that produce sound, including the voice, by the fact that it *propels* the shaman out of the body and off into the shamanic journey. It is truly a vehicle, a means of transport, and is often called a 'horse.' Like a horse, it may seem to have a life of its own, a temperament. In her research into shamanic drumming, Melinda Maxwell reports that 'In the oral tradition of Tuvinian shamans of Siberia, it is said that if the drum is nice, then the ritual works. If the drum if good, the shaman flies over the mountains and over very long distances. The soul goes out of the body, and the shaman begins to fly. If the drum is bad, the shaman stays on the ground.'[17]

How drumming has this effect is not fully understood. The typical shamanic drumbeat of 4 to 4 1/2 beats per second produces brain waves in the theta range, which are associated with threshold states of consciousness in the twilight zone just before waking or sleeping. It is a state of reverie, of drifting in and out of consciousness, often with startling, animated imagery, and sudden insights or illuminations. It is the brain-wave pattern found in experienced meditators, quickly leading to unconsciousness and sleep in the inexperienced. The theta range of brain waves is also the human equivalent of Earth's electromagnetic frequency of 7.5 cycles per second. The rhythm of the drum appears to enable shamans not merely to enter an altered state of consciousness but also to expand and align their consciousness with the pulse of planet Earth. A single drumbeat contains many low frequencies. The compounded effect of these beats, one after the other at the crucial rate, creates a pattern of frequencies that shifts the mind from its normal sequential functioning into a more timeless, spatial awareness. The sound of the drum is no longer perceived simply as a succession of beats. It starts to 'sing' with undertones and overtones, with an orchestration of sound that lifts the veil between the worlds, letting in more unearthly sounds, the sounds of the spirit world itself. As the bounds of normal consciousness are broken, the distinction between self and other dissolves, and it can seem as if the drum is drumming itself. American psychologist Carl Levett discovered this after buying himself a drum.

> ...one day while practicing I was shocked by the sudden realization that the drumming was coming not from me, but from somewhere else. I double-checked in disbelief, but it was a fact. The drumming continued in perfect rhythm, yet completely out of my control. Immediately my body began to convulse and energy surged from deep within me, becoming a liquid radiance which saturated every cell of my body. All conceptions I had of myself vanished as I dissolved into this flow.[18]

Again we see the rising of a liquid radiance, like the Bushman's *n/um*, the Australian karadji's *miwi*, and the Eastern mystic's *kundalini*, which loosens the grip of self-consciousness as it rises through the body. As consciousness separates from the body, the whole other world of 'non-ordinary reality' opens up – an expansive, metaphysical terrain through which the shaman journeys, transported by the beat of the drum.

The shaman's cosmos

Despite some variations between cultures, the universe which the shaman enters to negotiate with the spirits is usually layered into three cosmic zones—an upper, middle, and lower world. These levels correspond to the sky above, to everyday life on Earth, and an underworld below. The painted caves of ice age Europe, for example, would have provided our shamanic ancestors with physical access to the non-physical realms of the lower world, enabling them to make what Eliade has called 'the break-through in plane.'

The different regions of the shamanic cosmos have their own distinct character, colored by local traditions. In many cosmologies the lower world is the land of the dead, and to journey there may be both menacing and dangerous. But each region is interconnected by a central axis which allows the shaman to move up and down, between one and another. The axis might be seen as a mountain, a pillar, or a tree, which passes through an opening or a hole. It is through this opening that 'the gods descend to earth and the dead to the subterranean regions; it is through the same hole that the soul of the shaman in ecstasy can fly up or down in the course of his celestial or infernal journeys.'[19]

Amongst some tribal peoples, the structure of this cosmos is reflected in their dwellings and houses, where a central pillar reaches up through the smoke hole in the roof to the opening made by the Pole Star in the sky. The shaman's special gift is being able to enter these openings and traverse the worlds, whereas other people may only be able to use them to make offerings. Eliade links this central opening to the upper world with the widespread ancient belief in an age of innocence when direct communication between heaven and earth was possible. People had easier access to the gods and spirits in the upper regions, which was lost in the depths of time. With this loss of access, the shaman's ascent up the cosmic tree became the only way to maintain real communication with the inhabitants of these worlds.

Whilst journeys to the upper world might be exhilarating, involving contact with celestial beings, those to the lower world may be fraught with danger through encounters with evil spirits. Shamans also frequently undertake middle world journeys across Earth's geographical terrain, as it appears in everyday reality. They may have been asked to look for a missing person, or to carry out a distant healing. A middle world journey could even be into someone's body. 'The shamanic cosmos,' writes anthropologist Piers Vitebsky, 'is not only "out there" but is inside every one of us, and the shaman who journeys through the cosmos is also traveling through the community's own mental and physical space. Sometimes the correspondence goes further than simply referring to the community's familiar landscape and the shamanic voyage takes place entirely inside a patient's body.'[20] For example, Vitebsky has described how a Cuna shaman of Panama used his army of helper spirits on 'an emergency expedition' into a pregnant woman's womb in order to induce labor.

> The shaman sits under the sick woman's hammock and repeats at great length the steps by which the midwife sent for him, as if to make the patient relive precisely and vividly every step of her own pain. He then enumerates each helper spirit, called *nelegan*, in detail, and gives them special weapons and equipment: black beads, flame-colored beads, tiger bones, armadillo bones and silver necklaces, but especially their pointed, penetrating hats.[21]

As they enter the patient's vagina, the *negelans'* hats light up the route, and the shaman describes their itinerary through a landscape which is 'both the internal anatomy of a living body and an emotional geography of the psyche which inhabits it.' As they approach the womb, the *negelan* do battle with various spirits which have been preventing birth, using their pointed hats as weapons. Having overcome these spirits, the shaman must induce birth and 'summons further reinforcement such as the armadillo, a Lord of the Burrowing Animals.' The *negelan* must then widen the cervix and vaginal passage in order to draw the baby out behind them. 'Whereas on the inward journey the nelegan squeezed through in single file, on the return journey they come out marching four abreast.'[22]

The shamanic cosmos is clearly both intimate and immanent in the sense that it embraces and interpenetrates the physical space we live in. But it is also transcendent—hidden and remote—for it is accessible only to the shaman. This paradox represents not so much a misalignment between these worlds as in our consciousness of them. In Part I we saw how, at a critical time in our deep past, human consciousness contracted and 'fell in two.' The shaman's task is to bridge this gulf, or as Piers Vitebsky suggests, 'to return to some primordial state of grace. The shaman is a specialist in crossing this otherwise impassable gulf, and only a shaman has the necessary technique and the courage to do so.'[23]

In the many mythologies which tell of a lost paradise, it was not only heaven and earth which became separated. It was also our friendship with animals. People had once lived at peace with animals and understood their language. But after 'the fall from grace,' we became separated, as Joseph Campbell points out, 'in the awakened mind from the innocence, not only of the beasts without, but also of the beast within....'[24] An essential part of becoming a shaman is the genuinely religious quest to heal that split, both with 'the beast without' and 'the beast within.' The proliferation of animals in the Palaeolithic cave paintings, many of which were not hunted as food, testifies to this need. They were painted in ritual acts of spiritual reunion. The shamans were re-enacting a *participation mystique* which had once existed between human beings and animals, as well as absorbing their essences or qualities as spiritual beings. Like Vitebsky, Eliade sees the shamanic quest as a recovery of that lost innocence.

> While preparing for his ecstasy and during it, the shaman abolishes the present human condition and, for the time being, recovers the situation as it was at the beginning. Friendship with animals, knowledge of their language, transformation into an animal are so many signs that the shaman has re-established the "paradisal" situation lost at the dawn of time.[25]

This mystical reunion is not some abstract, airy pursuit, without consequences for everyday life. For the shaman is a practical mystic, and in that relationship with the 'beast within' lies their power to help and heal the ills of the tribe.

The power animal

Shamans believe that every human being has at least one guardian, a being from the spirit worlds who gives protection, strength, help, support, as well as maintaining good health and providing advice. In shamanic cultures this guardian spirit usually takes the form of an animal, with specific transcendent powers. The Yakuts of Siberia, for example, see this helping spirit both as an animal and also a 'fiery force.'

> Every shaman... must have an animal-mother or origin-animal. It is usually pictured in the form of an elk, less often as a bear. This animal lives independently, separated from the shaman. Perhaps it can best be imagined as the fiery force of the shaman that flies over the earth.... It is the embodiment of the prophetic gift of the shaman... it is the shaman's visionary power, which is able to penetrate both the past and the future.[26]

The shaman's animal guardian is generally known as the *power animal*. While a shaman may have one particular animal as their main ally, they may also be able to call upon a number of helping spirits, like the Cuna shaman with his *negelan*. These spirits are not always animals. They may be elemental spirits, like air, for example, which enables the shaman to pass through tight cracks in the earth when entering the underworld. Whatever their form, these allies bring their strengths to bear on the shaman's journeys, helping to deal with unpredictable and often difficult situations in the spirit worlds.

The actual 'power' of the animal guardian is primarily an impersonal, universal energy flowing through the web of creation. It takes on a particular configuration as the power animal, expressing certain qualities of the animal kingdom in relation to the shaman. The power animal is sometimes misunderstood in the West as if it were a symbol which may have the power to affect a person psychologically, but which is only in the mind. But the shaman's animal guardian is a real, independent being, incorporating the living energy of the whole of its species. It is not *a* Bear, *an* Eagle, or *a* Lion but *Bear, Eagle, Lion*, each representing the essential soul-group of that animal. Unlike a symbol which can be fed or programmed into the mind and then left, a shaman's animal ally must be attended to, sung to and danced with; otherwise it may wander off on its own, leaving the shaman vulnerable to illness, depression or despair. When attended to, it bestows its own unique powers or qualities upon the shaman, bringing them to bear upon the sacred tasks which he or she is called upon to perform. For example, *Lion* might bring the qualities of courage and skill in stalking prey to the search for food. *Eagle* might bring mastery of the air element, and grace, fluency, and power to the shaman during their magical flight through the spirit worlds.

While the main vehicle for shamanic flight may be drumming, the 'engine' of this vehicle — the enhanced energy needed to enter and traverse the spirit worlds — comes from the shaman's relationship with their power animal. It is an elemental energy, tapped by the shaman in tribal societies through their embeddedness within the natural world; these are societies in which animals are respected and sometimes revered for the powers or magical qualities they possess. This is power as understood by indigenous peoples who know and belong to their world, who recognize the land they share with the rest of creation as being imbued with soul, and animated by spirit.

In his book, *The Heart of the Hunter*, Laurens van der Post describes this sense of belonging which the Bushman always had in the vast wilderness of the Kalihari desert. 'Wherever he went he felt known, whatever he encountered, starlight, cloud, tree, or animal, knew him. I believe the Bushman's way to knowing was through what knew him.'[27] The Bushman still retained a certain access to the primal mind which has been lost to Western civilization, so that what they experienced in the outer world was reflected in their own inner nature. Their sensitivity was so finely tuned to the living presences in their world that their technology *was* their expanded awareness. For example, van der Post tells the story of a young Bushman who went out hunting one day and was overwhelmed by the desire to sleep.

> He climbed a hill to look about for game, and there to his surprise began to feel sleepy. He should have been warned by that: it was a notorious axiom among the first people that animals defended themselves against hunters by inducing sleep in them. A little animal induced a little sleep, a dangerous animal a great sleep. Even to this day in the Kalihari, the Bushman believes it, and this young man of the early race should have known that such a desire to sleep in the light of day could only have been caused by one of the greatest of animals... To give the image its modern idiom: the tendency to sleep represents the tendency to unawareness; our animal nature defends itself against the bows and arrows of the conscious mind by bringing darkness and unawareness to our spirit......So, when this young man is overwhelmed by sleepiness it is not surprising that a lion appears.[28]

For shamans, too, contact with their power animal cannot be achieved through the intellect alone. They may have to go through darkness, suffering and unawareness before it can approach them. But having established a relationship with this transcendent elemental being, they cultivate it, never attempting their magical flight into the highly-charged and often treacherous worlds of the spirits alone; and through the privileged position bestowed upon them by this special, other-worldly relationship, shamans are able to bring through the riches — the gifts, skills, healings and visions — from the worlds beyond the threshold of normal awareness into the social domain of the tribe.

CHAPTER 5

INITIATION AND THE TRIBE

Among my people, there is a saying that you don't find the spirit – the spirit finds you.
Johnny Moses, Northwest Coast Native American spiritual teacher[1]

The shaman is pre-eminently a technician of transcendence, a specialist, gifted with certain mystical abilities which set them apart from other members of the tribe. But this giftedness was traditionally nurtured by the community, so that the shaman-to-be could eventually fulfill their equally important, sacred role as the healer and spiritual guardian of tribal life. As Mircea Eliade has pointed out, '...shamanism is important not only for the place that it holds in the history of mysticism. The shamans have played an essential role in the defense of the psychic integrity of the community.'[2]

The shaman is a spiritual warrior, empowered by their natural ability to cross the threshold between worlds and manipulate energies in the transpersonal realms of the spirits. They might often be the only person in the tribe equipped with the knowledge and skills needed to battle against the forces of sickness and death assailing it from these worlds. As the guardian of the tribal soul, the shaman's power is dedicated to healing and binding the tribe together as a spiritually integrated whole.

The search for spirit
Every traditional shaman goes through some kind of initiation, a transformative experience that enables them to shed the skin of their former life and prepare for their new role in society. Depending upon local customs and traditions, the shaman may be elected and instructed by an older shaman, or their vocation may come unexpectedly as an 'affliction from the spirits.' Whether it is

deliberate, or more spontaneous, or a combination of the two, initiation will involve degrees of suffering. The young shaman undergoes ritual acts of endurance, social deprivation, and raw encounters with the elements on their quest for spiritual power. For, ultimately, it is through immersion in the numinous energies of the spirit worlds that they are transformed and empowered for their essential, sacred role in society.

In some tribal societies—especially North American—ordinary tribespeople, as well as the shaman-to-be, go on a special search for the power and giftedness, which contact with the spirit worlds can bring. Known as the 'vision quest,' this search might form part of normal rites of passage from adolescence to adulthood. The young person leaves their village and goes out into the wilderness, perhaps to a mountain or a hilltop, in order to pray for a vision. Involving varying degrees of hardship and isolation, the vision quest often lasts for just a few days. But it might also continue for weeks, months, and sometimes even years, until the person's guardian spirit makes itself known through a dream or a vision, usually in the form of an animal. What distinguishes the shaman-to-be from other people on the vision quest is the intensity of this search, and perhaps a natural inclination towards trance. Having made contact with the spirits, they develop this ability to enter 'non-ordinary reality' at will.

Typically the vision quest involves a strong sense of preparation. As Johnny Moses explains, one needs to make oneself ready to be chosen by the spirits.

> When we go on vision quests, it's not a question of where to go to find medicine power but whether we are ready to receive it. We know the spirits and ancestors are always there in the forests and the mountains, waiting for us to visit them—and, among our people, visiting is a sacred art.[3]

Before they leave the village the young person fasts and undergoes self-cleansing, physically, emotionally and spiritually. They might strip and enter a sweat lodge, which has been prepared for them by their family, or by the tribal medicine man or woman. Shaped like a bee-hive, made of branches, and covered with blankets, cloths or quilts, the sweat lodge contains a pit in its centre where a fire burns, heating rocks onto which water is poured. The rising steam might mingle perhaps with smoke from burning sage, which the young person inhales as part of this deeply symbolic and also physical act of purification. In many ways, the self-cleansing before the vision quest resembles the acts of self-purification carried out in other spiritual disciplines, where one makes oneself as pure a 'vessel' as possible to receive 'spirit.' And, as Johnny Moses points out, the rigors of preparing for the vision quest are also a demonstration of intent and purpose to the spirits, of a willingness to be chosen by them.

> We believe that people have to show the spirit that they really mean business, that they're strong enough to work with power. And, in medicine work, we have to suffer to make ourselves strong. The word for suffering in our language is not a negative thing; it refers to forces that are pressing or pushing on us that we can feel very strongly. Suffering helps us become strong so we can withstand the winds and storms of life.[4]

The everyday lives of most tribal peoples are lived tight against nature. This exposure to the elements is for them closeness to spirit, and the closer to spirit one comes the stronger one needs to be. In order to approach the spirits directly, the young person on the vision quest needs to strip away the comforts of everyday human life and discover their own inherent elemental strength, which they possess naturally through being themselves part of the natural world. With the spirits pressing in on them, they suffer, in the sense of shedding their human skin for a while, in order to experience the elemental power of Earth's spirit, and to hear what that spirit is telling them. Amongst Johnny Moses's ancestors, this kind of suffering and 'making oneself strong' was part of the upbringing of young people, and many Native American children begin their preparations for the vision quest as early as six years old.

Our people traditionally started preparing for the vision quest at a very young age. In some places they bathed in ice-cold water every day. They ate plant medicines and roots to cleanse their bodies. They practiced fasting and praying. Before they went out on vision quests to pray for medicine, they learned to sit up and stay awake for as long as they could. Even after that, people often had to wait quite a long time before they received power.[5]

Once out in the wilderness, the young person would be alone, perhaps for the first time after a childhood surrounded by the tribe. They might stay out only at night-time and return to the village in the morning, and this would go on until they had a dream or a vision of the spirit who would bring them power or their special giftedness from the spirit worlds. In the darkness of the wilderness night, they would be surrounded, not by the sounds of the sleeping village, but by the rawness of nature alive. There might be a loosening of their normal sense of self, and a crossing of the threshold between worlds into non-ordinary reality. Lakota shaman, Lame Deer, describes this experience, alone on a hilltop at night.

> Blackness was wrapped around me like a velvet cloth. It seemed to cut me off from the outside world, even from my own body. It made me listen to the voices within me.....Sounds came to me through the darkness: the cries of the wind, the whisper of the trees, the voices of nature, animal sounds, the hooting of an owl. Suddenly I felt an overwhelming presence. Down there with me in my cramped hole was a big bird. The pit was only as wide as myself, and I was a skinny boy, but that huge bird was flying around me as if he had the whole sky to himself.[6]

The meeting with the power animal, or other guardian spirit, is the decisive event on the path towards becoming a shaman, for it is the moment at which real and direct contact with the world of the spirits is established. The shaman will develop an intense relationship with the power animal, since it is their connection with the power of the transpersonal realms. It provides, in a sense, the psychic thrust, or energy, which the shaman needs in order to deliberately propel their consciousness out of their body and into the worlds of the spirits. This is what sets the shaman apart from ordinary members of the tribe. While they too may contact a power animal or other guardian spirit on their vision quest, as Johnny Moses points out, this may have more to do with discovering the qualities or talents which enable them to make their own unique contribution to the community.

> A spirit power doesn't have to be an animal power; it can also be what in Western society would be called a talent or a profession. For example, in our area, people usually receive the drum as a gift in a dream or have a special calling before they begin to play the drum. Other people receive hunting or fishing gifts, or a cooking medicine. In the Northwest Coast, such gifts are considered spirit helpers.7

For the Native American, the vision quest is a rite of passage which may lead to the discovery of what is unique about a person, to what inspires them, to a revelation of their special abilities. As an aspect of initiation, it may or may not result in a person becoming a fully-fledged shaman. But it does reflect the orientation of many tribal peoples towards the individual—as someone belonging to the community, but also possessing their own unique gifts or talents, which in turn are nurtured for the benefit of both the individual and the tribe.

The wounding crisis
Suffering is implied in the word *shaman*, as one who 'practices austerities,' as well as in the expression, the 'wounded healer,' for the encounter with psychological and physical suffering is the most common and well-known route to becoming a shaman in tribal societies, although it is not the only one. A person may be

born with the power to contact spirits and to heal, or the gift may manifest spontaneously, often through a dream. Equally it may appear, as we have seen, during the vision quest in the course of normal initiation rites.

While this more deliberate approach to the spirits may identify a young shaman's vocation, perhaps the most authentic manner of initiation is through a wounding crisis which disables the individual in such a way that they cannot follow the conventional adult path through life, normally trodden by members of their tribe. They may have been maimed, suffered a serious illness, or nearly died. By being brought closer to death, they experience the immanence of awesome, transcendent forces beyond their control. And it is this contact with the other worlds, causing a shift in their perception of what is real, that precipitates a psychospiritual crisis. The person becomes temporarily unbalanced or disturbed, unable to participate in the life of their community. They may spend nights weeping, and dreaming of impending death, of being imprisoned in the underworld, or chased and devoured by animals. Their life becomes chaotic, as they slip in and out of ordinary consciousness. They become *immune* in the original sense of the word—'exempt from public service.' They are not required to go hunting or to engage in the other communal activities which ensure the smooth running of tribal life. They are allowed to enter fully into the reality of their experience, perhaps guided through the crisis by an older shaman. They become more acquainted with the turbulent astral energies surrounding them, and with the transcendent beings which are visiting them. They make contact and become familiar with their guardian spirit—frequently a power animal—and, as they do so, they learn to handle these difficult energies and to actively explore the transcendent realms.

The wounding crisis may well be visited upon an individual who is already particularly raw—more thin-skinned, sensitive, and intuitive than most—perhaps with a tendency towards trance. It is as if, through the wound, there lies an opening into the universe at large, a universe closed to the average person. Moving into this universe may at first be overwhelming, but because members of the tribe understand and respect the purpose of this calling, they are able collectively to contain the disruption caused by the individual's shift in psychic and spiritual orientation. The transformative experience of break-down, crisis, and initiation, takes place in a supportive context where the vulnerability of this tender-mindedness and sensitivity is valued as an asset, since members of the tribe know that their survival may ultimately depend upon the ability of the shaman to tap into the invisible worlds for information and healing.

While in our society a crisis like this might be treated as pathological, and the person labeled 'psychotic,' in shamanic communities it is viewed, not as an illness, but as a unique event of its own kind. It is seen as a vocation in the true sense of the word, since the spirits are calling to the person in crisis to move away from the concerns of ordinary life and to become active in the metaphysical domain of the worlds beyond. The young person is struck and overwhelmed by a sense of the sacred, by the immanence of the divine, both in themselves and in the world around them. There is often a sense of urgency to seek solitude, and they might become temporarily isolated and even estranged from the community. Divorced from the concerns of everyday life, they seek out the wilderness, both the vast, unpopulated expanses of the natural world, and the deep, unexplored spaces of their inner world, one reflecting the other. Alone and open to the elements, the boundary between the wilderness within and the natural world around them begins to dissolve, as they enter the embrace of Earth's mythic and spiritual dimension. Stones, trees, rivers, animals, all begin to speak to them in voices that their awakening natural spirit hears and understands. In each encounter, the young shaman experiences the Great Spirit that animates all the myriad expressions of life, binding them to Earth and to each other.

In the solitude of the wilderness, the shaman-to-be no longer feels alone. In their dreaming and in their wakefulness, images and objects reveal the animating essence which underlies their mere appearances. Dream images are seen as real beings, spirits populating the mythic reality which the young person is entering, a reality which becomes for them perhaps more real than normal, everyday life.

As Holger Kalweit says of this entry through solitude into the mythic and metaphysical dimension, 'While we interact to become more human, shamans learn humanity through solitude. Having only themselves to rely on and shut off from society, they abandon themselves ascetically to their aloneness. Because they have left others' approaches to the world behind and have become loners, they must be alone. Their new friends and companions belong to another dimension.'[8]

Guardian of the tribal soul
Amongst indigenous peoples, the shaman has always been the spiritual focus, or 'hearth,' of tribal life. During the long frozen millennia of the last ice age, and right up to the present day, it is as if the shaman has kept *the living flame of the spirit burning* for the whole of tribal humanity, maintaining its spiritual cohesion and fighting for its survival. Shamanism is very much about survival, both the spiritual and physical survival of the tribe. It became the task or role of this often wounded but gifted tribal person, whom we now call 'shaman,' to bridge the everyday visible world with the invisible worlds of transpersonal forces which permeate everyday life. And their purpose has always been the same, to establish balance within individuals needing healing, balance within their community, and balance between the human community and all other forms of life on the planet, of which the human race is but one.

Although the wilderness experience and solitude of shamanic initiation entails the separation of the shaman-to-be from their community, this social isolation is sanctioned and accepted by the tribe. For the crisis is not an opting out for its own sake, but an opting out in order to find a deeper experience of life. The break with society becomes necessary as the individual on the path of initiation becomes less and less able to tolerate the seeming superficiality of everyday concerns, for the universe is calling them to enter into the world beyond appearances, where the energies which influence health and sickness, and life and death, are encountered directly. Unlike the apparently pointless suffering of much modern mental illness, the shaman's passage through pain acquires meaning, at first through their contact with the metaphysical worlds, but then also through dedicating their spiritual power to healing, helping and defending the tribe. While the wounding, or spiritual crisis, undergone by the shaman may draw them initially away from the tribe, they cultivate a sense of separateness, not out of a narcissistic need to be different, but in the knowledge that only through faithful attention to their calling from the spirits can they serve the deepest needs of their community.

Many shamans return to the tribe after initiation to carry on a normal occupation. But they are commonly perceived as being different, belonging, in a sense, to the world of the spirits; and they are acknowledged as holding a privileged position within society. This privilege entails no less a responsibility than maintaining the psychic integrity of the tribe in a balanced relationship with all the worlds, both visible and invisible, around them. They will have to administer not only the souls and spirits of individual tribespeople, but also the collective soul and spirit of the tribe as a whole.

As Eliade says of the shamans throughout human history, 'This small mystical elite not only directs the community's religious life but, as it were, guards its "soul." The shaman is the great specialist in the human soul; he alone "sees" it, for he knows its "form" and its destiny.'[9] While much of the everyday religious life of the community may be orchestrated by other spiritual leaders or priests, the shaman is called upon to be the spiritual troubleshooter, whenever issues of health, illness, life, death, and survival arise. They alone have 'died' in order to journey into the spirit worlds, and they alone have the special skills to negotiate successfully with the beings which inhabit these metaphysical realms.

This direct line to the spirits also means that the shaman is the prime source of inspiration from the spirit worlds, a cultural force animating and invigorating the tribe, ensuring its survival through spiritual growth and cultural development. This is apparent, for example, in James Cowan's description of the Australian *karadji*, or 'clever man.'

> Because of his direct contact with the Dreaming and its pantheon of spirit-figures, he was one of the few people able to create new dances, songs and stories. Through him a tribal community could remain culturally vital and grow accordingly.[10]

It is as if, through the kindling and stoking of their own inner fire, shamans and medicine men, like the *karadji*, become the spiritual focus for the collective—a 'living flame'—creating a centering warmth, or spiritual hearth, through which the group finds a sense of unity and coherence, held together under its radiant glow. The shaman is a *political force* within communities which understand that political power is first and foremost sacred and spiritual and only in a secondary sense secular. For these communities, all of life—birth, death, the cycle of the seasons, finding food and shelter, relationships within the group, and with other tribes—is imbued with the sacred; and all activities are acknowledged as being influenced by invisible spiritual energies which lie beyond the reach of the average person who has not undergone the shamanic crisis and initiation.

The essence of tribal shamanism lies not only within the psychic turmoil and spiritual transformation of the individual passing through the shamanic crisis. It is also rooted within the community itself, which embraces and supports the initiatory event. As a practical mystic, the shaman possesses the inner luminosity of their 'seeing,' and the ecstatic flight of their journeying. But these are experiences which other people in mainstream culture can and do have—as seers, prophets, poets, visionaries, artists, musicians, psychics, and spiritual seekers. What defines the tribal shaman over and above the inner experience of personal transformation, and empowerment through contact with spirits, is the *embrace of the tribe*. The shared understanding with their tribe—over the nature of their suffering and the purpose of their calling — provides the shaman-to-be with the firm social ground for them to enact their role later on, as guardian of the tribal soul.

CHAPTER 6

THRESHOLDS BETWEEN WORLDS

....hell is the spirit prevented from going on, it is time arrested in the nothingness between two states of being.
Laurens van der Post, The Heart of the Hunter[1]

For some people, life is punctuated by crises which can be managed, and which eventually pass like a storm. Business continues as usual, and the appearance of normality prevails. But for others, crisis precipitates collapse, which may herald the transition from a known to an unknown world. In the last chapter we saw how, for many tribal peoples, this more catastrophic collapse—psychological breakdown, a serious illness perhaps, or an accident—may be the first step on the initiatory path towards becoming a shaman. The individual is plunged into a journey of chaos, pain, psychic disintegration, and social isolation. But it may also be a journey of inner exploration and self-healing. The crisis and suffering are often recognized by members of the tribe as the sign of a vocation, as an opportunity for the young person to develop the special skills of the shaman. Through their inner turmoil and disruptive experience, they make contact with the spirits. A resurrection takes place, a reconstitution, out of which emerges a new, spiritually empowered person. Reborn back into the heart of tribal life, they return to serve their community, not so much as the 'wounded healer,' as 'the healed healer,' or shaman.

In the modern, developed world, catastrophic collapse too often plunges an unsupported young person into long-term psychosis, perhaps drug abuse, or crime. It is rarely viewed as an opportunity to develop whatever is unique about that person, and their suffering is seen as a social burden, a liability, threatening and costly to society. In our more rootless culture, in which invisible worlds are generally denied as non-existent, the richness of experience from the inner life goes untapped, and the individual's true gifts are consigned to the scrap-heap.

The crisis of shamanic initiation, although frequently painful and disruptive, is an expression of our fundamental, human need for spiritual growth, and of our longing for transcendence. It is a need which is generally honored by tribal peoples in their traditional rites of passage, which assist individuals on their path of development. The rites are cultural markers, signifying to the community as a whole that the individual is emerging into a new phase of life and perhaps a new role in society. They may also help a person to discover what it is that makes them unique, what their special gifts or talents are; and these are nurtured by the tribe for the contribution they can make to the community as a whole.

But the calling 'from the spirits' is by no means confined to tribal societies. The human spirit's need to evolve and move on is universal. When this need goes unrecognized, or is blocked, it can leave the individual stuck 'in the nothingness between two states of being,' on the threshold between worlds. The person may experience the hell of 'the spirit prevented from going on.' If their suffering becomes too acute or disruptive, they may be classified as 'mentally ill.'

Spiritual emergency

Of course, not all mental illness in our society is a thwarted shamanic impulse, or even the symptom of repressed talents or gifts. Far from it. Many psychiatric disorders have a genuine, detectable, physical origin, such as organic impairment, or a disease of the brain. Others have no detectable, physical basis, but the person may have failed to develop a sufficiently strong and coherent sense of self during their formative years. With the onset of crisis, their sense of self disintegrates, leaving a black hole in their psyche that becomes an open channel for negative and often violent energies. They may be overwhelmed by constant terror, and their behavior becomes destructive towards others or themselves. With such extreme suffering, and with no possibility of their gaining insight into their condition, people with mental illness of this kind need to be treated medically — in the absence of an alternative — by the use of suppressive drugs.

By contrast, there are many people who suffer mental breakdown or acute psychotic episodes, in which the blocking of an impulse towards personal growth and inner development is the primary, underlying cause of collapse. This is especially so at critical life junctures like the threshold between adolescence and adulthood. The individual needs to shed the skin of a previous life cycle in order to move on into a new, and perhaps more challenging one. Christina and Stanislav Grof, in their book, *The Stormy Search For The Self*, describe this process of growth as 'spiritual emergence.'

> In the most general terms, spiritual *emergence* can be defined as the movement of an individual to a more expanded way of being that involves enhanced emotional and psychosomatic health, greater freedom of personal choices, and a sense of deeper connection with other people, nature, and the cosmos. An important part of this development is an increasing awareness of the spiritual dimension in one's life...'[2]

All spiritual growth involves a degree of pain, since it is an ongoing process of dying to the old, and being born into the new. But sometimes this growth accelerates very rapidly, like new shoots appearing on a plant overnight. A person undergoes sudden and very painful inner change, producing what the Grofs call a 'spiritual emergency.' This play on words points both to the crisis produced by this acceleration of growth, and also to the opportunity to emerge into a new, previously unknown state of being. The individual experiences *a radical intensification of their inner life*. Like the turmoil of the shamanic crisis, this can make normal, everyday life either difficult or impossible to live. The inner experiences can be very disturbing, and since they often manifest as deeply introverted isolation, or as disruptive, even violent behavior, they not only resemble the turmoil of the shamanic crisis in tribal societies, they are also easily confused with the symptoms of acute, paranoid schizophrenia in our Western culture. Joan Halifax has also observed this similarity between the shamanic crisis of initiation and some of the symptoms of schizophrenia.

> Both shamans and schizophrenics often become caught up in a circle of ideas, omens, and objects. This obsessiveness gives rise to sleeplessness, where the boundary between the sleeping state and the waking state breaks down, plunging the individual into a twilight zone....
>
> Both schizophrenics and shaman-neophytes encounter death on the symbolic level, and frequently this encounter with death is preceded by an experience of dismemberment. Soul journeys and spirit voices also accompany this phase of the breakdown, as do ideas of world catastrophe, conspiracy theories, and missions of great importance.[3]

In both the shamanic and schizophrenic crisis, the individual is undergoing a psychic and spiritual death. They are being drawn into an underworld of experience, a world of astral energies, which seem to tear them apart. This psychic dismemberment heralds a death for the ordinary, everyday self, and is an archetypal experience in its own right, translated in our own culture into fairy tales, religious myth, and legend. But in shamanic initiation, the tribe may seek to deepen the disturbed individual's inner, mystical experiences through the use of ritual, and perhaps through the 'practice of austerities,' or drugs. Their crisis is culturally sanctioned and contained by a community which accepts their disruptive experiences as valuable contact with the powerfully *real* worlds of spirit. The 'land of the dead' and the worlds beyond are understood as possessing a numinous power, stronger, and in a sense more real or potent than the world of the living; and members of the tribe realize that access to the spirits may be vital for their survival. Everything is done to assist and instruct the young shaman in the ways of the spirit, and to ensure that they emerge from their experience of symbolic death reborn as a new and empowered person, as a practical mystic, capable of negotiating the spirit worlds on behalf of the tribe.

In Western society this rarely happens, for, as Joseph Campbell once put it, 'the schizophrenic is drowning in the same water in which the mystic is swimming in delight.'[4] Great efforts are made to suppress the disturbing experiences of psychosis in our culture. Lacking the spiritual awareness of tribal peoples, the modern, scientific mind can only see them as a malfunction of the brain's chemistry. The inner life of the person undergoing a schizophrenic crisis is viewed with bewilderment, and their behavior in the outer world is often treated with hostility. Normally, they are given suppressive drugs, which may make life more manageable in the short-term, but in the long-term obscure the real nature of the breakdown. For, as the Grofs have discovered, there are certain characteristics of the spiritual emergency that distinguish it from the kind of severe psychosis in need of medication. As in the initiatory crisis of the tribal shaman, the person undergoing the emergency will be aware that their experience has a transpersonal or spiritual dimension, despite their suffering. Another important hallmark of the spiritual emergency, observed by the Grofs, is 'the ability to differentiate to a *considerable* degree between inner experiences and the world of consensus reality.'[5] This is absent in people suffering from severe paranoid schizophrenia, who generally project the causes of their disturbing experiences outside of themselves, onto supposedly hostile others. They desperately lack self-awareness. By contrast, a person going through a spiritual emergency, with symptoms resembling psychosis like 'hearing voices,' would still retain the awareness that their disturbing experiences are part of their own internal process.

In our culture, we desperately need to stop blocking the disruptive aspects of personal growth and development. We especially need to find deeper understanding of the turmoil which young people often go through when they seem to be impelled upon a path that deviates from the comfortable norm. We have seen how the Native American vision quest deliberately encourages a young person on the threshold of adulthood to discover their own special giftedness, whatever it may be. This is not a purely narcissistic quest but a process which is part of tribal spirituality, one which feeds back directly into the community, so that the individual's specialness is also a means of contributing and belonging to society.

The modern, Western world needs to learn again how to mark and celebrate the individual's passage from one cycle of life to another, and to honor, equally, the processes of decay and death, as well as growth and renewal. For it only by allowing a person to let go, or die to their former self, that they can discover their new emerging talents or giftedness. We come to realize that their passage towards their own empowerment may need to be completed, like the fallen seed entering the earth, through darkness, disruption, and perhaps pain. Only then will we be able to assist and support the person in crisis with compassion and understanding. Through a deeper understanding of the nature of their suffering, we may be inspired to create new rites of passage, ones which honor our fundamental spiritual need to shed the past and move on into the future.

Just as the shaman's experience of initiation deepens their understanding of life and death, it can also help us to go more deeply into our own personal journeys, as we move through life from one phase to another. And the strength which the shaman gains from their socially endorsed passage through suffering could help us to look with greater awareness and a more open heart upon similar suffering which individuals go through in our own society.

The solitude of shamanic awakening

Like the shaman-to-be in tribal societies, there are people in our mainstream culture who also have, without doubt, a shamanic calling. They may undergo a spiritual emergency, or other experiences that resemble aspects of the initiatory crisis in tribal societies. They might suffer some form of catastrophic collapse, like an accident, the loss of a limb, a serious illness, or a wounding which brings them close to death. They, too, may seek solitude through which they become more aware, both of their woundedness, and also of their need for healing. But without traditional rites of passage in our culture, the calling is usually suppressed, so that it is only by 'chance,' or 'destiny,' that this kind of disabling crisis leads the individual into an exploration of their inner worlds and the process of spiritual awakening. When this happens, it represents a calling or summons from the transpersonal domain for the person to cross the thresholds between worlds — to expand their awareness and begin the search for their soul. It is a calling to actively seek out a broader, deeper experience of life, and to journey into the unknown. They may be drawn into the realms of dream consciousness, into the astral or spirit worlds, and in these realms they experience the presence of beings that are normally invisible to the outer eye.

Their spiritual awakening becomes especially shamanic if there is contact with animal guardians or other similarly elemental energies, which bring guidance and support on journeys through the shamanic universe.

Like the tribal shaman-to-be, for the Western person undergoing this shamanic awakening, it is through solitude that they make contact with the deepest levels of their being and find strength and healing. Inwardly, the space entered during solitude may be likened to a vast, inner shrine or sacred wilderness that possesses the tremendously fertile creativity of all that is dark, vague, shadowy and numinous, offering a path to the well-spring of the dream-life itself. This is solitude as a way of being, setting the individual apart from their community. It is the months- or even years-long immersion in an alternate, mythical reality — a movement into the creative womb of darkness. The individual enters a massive, nebulous, inner terrain of dark and undifferentiated forces.

Psychologically, solitude may involve confrontation with the dark, negative feminine — the black goddess — both fertile and abundant, but also potentially stagnant and destructive, like an octopus which clasps on, dragging one down to death by drowning. It is here that a person may experience panic and face the terror that surrounds the dark and unknown, as the awesome powers of nature and the amorality of instinct awaken. James Hillman has described this confrontation with fear.

> Panic, especially at night, when the citadel darkens and the heroic ego sleeps, is a direct participation mystique in nature, a fundamental, even ontological experience of the world as alive and in dread. Objects become subjects; they move with life while one is oneself paralyzed with fear. When existence is experienced through instinctual levels of fear, aggression, hunger or sexuality, images take on a compelling life of their own.[6]

From within the darkness nature comes alive and speaks to the person directly, especially in their dreams. They are drawn irrevocably into an awareness of the forces which lie beyond their conscious control. They hear the voices that would speak to them at all times if they but had ears to hear them. Intellect is suspended or replaced by an attentiveness through which they learn to ride the subtle currents of energies that interpenetrate the dimensions of both ordinary life and dream reality. They sense the rhythmical tidal pull of dream consciousness and learn to distinguish whether they are entering a shamanic state of consciousness at will, as the fully-empowered shaman does, or whether they are being caught in the undertow of astral energies and being dragged down to the sea bed, as happens *in extremis* during psychosis. With attentiveness they learn the fine line between escape into the astral worlds from the pressures of daily life, and deliberately journeying into them in order to bring back something of value.

It is through solitude, through the creative withdrawal into darkness—often experienced as the deep blackness of depression—that the person undergoing a shamanic awakening can give true dedication to the inner life. Dream reality is known and experienced to be real, perhaps even more so than ordinary waking life, so that what were once mere images move closer, spring to life, and communicate their presence, becoming livelier than life and presenting their own unique wisdom or humor. Like a love affair or a true calling, the richness of the inner life is cultivated by gentle attentiveness and the suspension of judgement. James Hillman calls it the 'faithful attention to the imaginal world,' a love which 'transforms mere images into presences, gives them living being, or rather reveals the living being which they do naturally contain... Psychic contents become powers, spirits, gods. One senses their presence as did all earlier people who still had soul.'[7]

'Faithful attention' to the inner wilderness, nurtured by solitude, is crucial for the awakening, modern shaman, if they are to sense the presence of their spirit helpers and harness their powers, for they are awakening to the reality of the spirit world, to its living being, which brings strength and healing to them. And while our largely urban society lacks an experience of the outer wilderness available to most tribal peoples, it is through contact with the non-human, elemental aspect of our *inner wilderness* that we become truly empowered.

Both the tribal and the modern, Western shaman set off on a journey beyond the purely personal domain of the psyche into the 'great plain of the spirit' — into the soul of nature itself. Enveloped in its numinous power, they reawaken to that deep sense of participation and belonging, which the human spirit has at its foundation with Earth's spirit. They experience Earth's energy as a vital force, as the living spirit flowing through and between all forms of life. Through solitude and wilderness, the shaman-to-be taps the primal human awareness of the power that dwells in all things, of the undifferentiated 'ultimate ground' of experience. An Alaskan shaman, called Najagneq, told the Arctic explorer, Knud Rasmussen about this power.

> ...a power that we call Sila, one that cannot be explained in so many words. A strong spirit, the upholder of the universe, of the weather, in fact all life on earth — so mighty that his speech to man comes not through ordinary words, but through storms, snowfall, rain showers, the tempests of the sea, through all the

forces that man fears, or through sunshine, calm seas, or small, innocent, playing children who understand nothing....No one has ever seen Sila. His place of sojourn is so mysterious that he is with us and infinitely far away at the same time.[8]

The mysterious Sila is, for Najagneq, 'the inhabitant or soul...of the universe.' As he told Rasmussen, 'All we know is that it has a gentle voice like a woman, a voice so fine and gentle that even children cannot become afraid. What it says is:...be not afraid of the universe.'[9]

Through the dark passage of initiation, the tribal shaman learns to face fear and death, and in doing so, gains access to the wider spiritual dimension. They become aware of the 'soul of the universe.' Similarly, in our mainstream culture, we need to face our collective fear, the fear of death and of letting go of ourselves. Our modern world is in the throes of a great metamorphosis between two states of being, a transformation of consciousness perhaps without precedent in recorded history. Like the tribal shaman going through the turbulence of initiation, it is as if we are undergoing the turmoil of a collective passage into a new and unknown world. The initiation of the shaman—with their separation from the tribe, their empowerment through contact with the transpersonal domain, and their reintegration with the tribe—can be both a guide and also a symbol for our collective, global journey through turmoil and transformation to a new level of human awareness, and a more integrated world. We need to expand our understanding and awareness of who we are into the unknown, and in doing so, we, too, may learn not to be afraid of the universe.

CHAPTER 7

THE NEW AGE SHAMAN

...in ways unimaginable to most of our ancestors, we are living in a world in which transformation has become one of the dominant characteristics. This is one reason, I believe, that we can talk about a New Age and how a sense of planetary transformation exists in our culture.
David Spangler, *Reimagination Of The World*[1]

The New Age

Many people live today with a strong, growing sense of expectation, as if some radical and rapid process of change has been activated, involving a fundamental break with the past, which will release us into a new and unknown future. The speed and extent of global transformation in the outer world is plain for all to see. But the magnitude of change within the human psyche is especially apparent to visionaries and mystics like David Spangler, who believes that 'the whole twentieth century and the first part of the twenty-first represent a vast metamorphosis of human consciousness and behavior whose only historical equivalent would be the invention of agriculture and the rise of civilization itself thousands of years ago.'[2]

It is as if the Western psyche has been struggling to emerge—like a butterfly from a chrysalis—from an ice age of the spirit. As the ice melts, and the human spirit is finally released from millennia of isolation, the embryonic stirrings of a more holistic, spiritual awareness from the last quarter of the 20th century become the fully-fledged incarnation of a New Age consciousness. What I mean here by 'New Age' is the spiritual awakening which was already being ushered in two hundred years ago by visionaries like William Blake who believed that 'what was going to come to pass was a gradual reversal of premises...the basis of reality would again be seen as spirit and not matter.'[3] David

Spangler sees the New Age as 'the capacity of both an individual and a culture to transform, to experience *metanoia* – or a radical change of mind.'[4] For him, it is very much an inner phenomenon, a process of 'inner reorganization' which allows a greater wholeness to manifest in our world. He defines the New Age as 'that inner place where we touch our own boundaries and accept transformation into our lives as a creative, natural and organic part of living. It is the place of our co-creativity and our deepening attunement to a larger wholeness.'[5]

A transformation is taking place within the Western psyche as a whole, and an important part of this great renaissance of spirit is the reawakening of our indigenous sense of belonging to Earth. It is, literally, a 're-membering,' with the possibility to re-connect in fuller, more mature awareness with our eclipsed primal spirit. The need is being recognized collectively within our culture for a more instinctual approach to spirituality, along with the individual need for self-empowerment. Together these needs have been rekindling the embers of shamanic consciousness, left smoldering from the onslaught of religion, science, and more recently, the soulless ethos of mass consumerism.

Many people see tribal spirituality and the practices of shamanism as a way of introducing a more Earth-based, instinctual sense of the sacred back into their lives; and they may embrace shamanism as a path to re-membering or rediscovering their vital inner connection to the natural universe. Medical anthropologist Joan Halifax, a long-time student of both ancient and modern shamanism, sees a similar motivation behind the Western shamanic quest.

> The initiatory and visionary experiences of the shaman, as well as the practical methods used to achieve them, are thought by many to offer a possible key to psychospiritual reintegration, while the shamanic world view appears to provide a possible basis for reharmonizing our now out-of-balance relationship with nature and the Earth.[6]

Shamanism has become very much part of New Age spirituality. But the manner in which we approach shamanic practices is crucial to whether we experience greater psychospiritual integration, or further disintegration. The revival of ancient rituals or other spiritual practices from the past may provide some people with the vehicle for their transition to a new awareness. But for others, these practices may trigger, not so much a radical change of mind, as an atavistic return to the past. They may become aware of their tribal 'past lives' and experience a pull from the past which makes it difficult for them to integrate their inner experience with their outer, worldly lives.

The motivation towards shamanism in our culture is often urgent and deeply sincere. But we need to ask whether its ancient practices are relevant to us today. Is there a place in modern society for the New Age shaman?

Which way of the shaman?

During the heady days of the 1960s, two anthropologists, Carlos Castaneda and Michael Harner, were laying the foundations for what would become the revival of shamanism in mainstream Western society. Individually, they were poles apart in their attitudes towards shamanism. Castaneda always emphasized the inaccessibility of the shaman's world for people not belonging to a shamanic culture. Even in his last comments before his death in 1998, Castaneda continued to shroud shamanism in mystery.

> I have never been able to draw conclusions about shamanism because in order to do this one needs to be an active member in the shaman's world.....One needs a lifetime to be able to acquire membership in a cultural world. I've been working for more than thirty years in the cognitive world of the shamans of ancient Mexico and, sincerely, I don't believe that I have acquired the membership that would allow me to draw conclusions or even propose them.[7]

Harner, by contrast, has been concerned to demystify shamanism.

'I saw that the ancient knowledge of shamanism was in danger of being lost as modern civilization made further and further inroads into native cultures. I wanted to give people an opportunity to reclaim their ancient heritage.'[8] Having immersed himself in the shamanism of native peoples in the Ecuadoran Andes and the Peruvian Amazon, Harner believes that anyone can learn to access a shamanic state of consciousness, whether they belong to a tribal society or not.

Both Castaneda and Harner went beyond the normal detached objectivity of academic anthropology by apprenticing themselves to shamans and learning the way of the shaman first-hand. But while Castaneda created a modern, romantic myth of the 'impeccable shaman' in the form of his legendary mentor, the Yaqui Indian sorcerer, don Juan, Harner's concern has been more evangelical. He believes that time is running out for the world to be saved from the forces of destruction. He feels we cannot afford the more leisurely approach to spirit which tribal peoples have always had. We in the West must be awakened as quickly as possible to the connectedness of all things, or else we might 'sleep forever.'

Both Castaneda and Harner have had an enormous impact upon the New Age movement as it has struggled to find and express a more instinctual spirituality. Each in his own way has touched, and perhaps awoken in our consciousness, the archetype of the shaman.

'An extremely sober shaman'

Castaneda's enigmatic books, describing his apprenticeship with don Juan, fired the collective imagination of a generation seeking alternative ways of being and seeing in a world which had become corrupted by science, religion and the corporate vested interests of industrialists and politicians. The teachings of don Juan were personal, mysterious and dramatic, opening a window onto an alternate reality which was infinitely rich and perilous. A far cry from the more rarefied spirituality of some traditional religions, don Juan's universe was strange, colorful, unpredictable, terrifyingly chaotic, and could only be negotiated through moral stamina, courage and self-discipline.

> Shamans like don Juan are essentially practical. For them there only exists a predatory universe where intelligence or awareness is the product of life and death challenges. He considered himself a navigator of infinity and said that in order to navigate into the unknown like a shaman does, one needs unlimited pragmatism, boundless sobriety and "guts of steel." In view of all this, don Juan believed that "spirituality" is simply a description of something impossible to achieve within the patterns of the world of everyday life, and it is not a real way of acting.[9]

Unlike the tribal shaman, don Juan embodies the spirit of modern mystical individualism, seeking out experience in an alternate reality, not in order to serve the community, but as part of one's own personal process—in the search for freedom. Don Juan's teachings are, in a sense, a map drawn by a modern mystic, rather than a description of the traditional shaman's world. Don Juan tells Castaneda that 'the true goal of dreaming is to perfect the energy body,'[10] a goal very similar perhaps to that of the mystic pushing experience of the inner worlds to its limits, and undergoing continual self-refinement in order to achieve ultimate union with the infinite. Also unlike the tribal shaman, don Juan is concerned to move away from 'the obsessive fixation of the mind on practices and techniques, the unwarranted influence over people.'[11] The tribal shaman, by definition, uses practices and techniques when helping members of the tribe, and is bound to have varying degrees of influence over people through the very nature of their role in society.

Don Juan's search, by contrast, is the search for freedom, '...freedom to perceive, without obsessions, all that's humanly possible.'[12] The tribe does not come into the equation. Modern sorcerers, he says, have 'no interest in concrete gains. There are no social functions for them, as there were for the sorcerers of the past.'[13] Instead of the rituals of tribal shamanism, don Juan recommends certain ways of being — like 'living impeccably,' 'losing self-importance,' and 'erasing personal history' — in order to navigate the unknown successfully, and to perceive all that's humanly possible. Some of these recommendations, such as losing self-importance and erasing personal history, would be familiar to mystics in all times and in all places.

The teachings of don Juan are a unique record of a long, idiosyncratic inner journey. Some consider them largely fictional, but this is irrelevant to the effect that they have had as a catalyst for cultural change and personal transformation. They have presented a radical psychospiritual formula for a generation with an urgent need both to blast off into inner space, and also to find a new set of guidelines to live by. But, in a sense, they stop short — they stay within the magical world of don Juan without connecting to ordinary reality. They soar to the heights of inner experience, but remain at odds with the everyday world. The emphasis is upon action and performance in non-ordinary reality, with an apparent lack of concern about other people, of the need to live with them, or to act on their behalf. They portray an essentially self-referential, perhaps narcissistic universe. There is no interest, for example, in healing — the primary role of the tribal shaman — and the energy body is described less in terms of what it can do for others and more like a high-powered performance vehicle, which can transport itself in an instant to the ends of the universe. Castaneda has said that 'the goal of don Juan's shamanism is to break the parameters of historical and everyday perception,'[14] and his books do this by throwing our normal understanding of reality into turmoil. Once our parameters of everyday perception have been broken, the teachings also offer a way to go about rewiring ourselves in order to achieve a new way of viewing the world that transcends the use of intellect.

Castaneda's books may be viewed as a blend of mystical or 'astral' escapism and moral self-improvement. For given his own enigmatic personality, along with the inaccessibility of the shamanic universe portrayed, we are left essentially with a simple set of recommendations about how to develop ourselves in the pursuit of spiritual freedom, recommendations which can be found within other approaches to spirituality. Yet the influence of Castaneda's books has been immeasurable in creating a modern romantic image of the shaman as one who acts 'impeccably.' Don Juan remains cool and invulnerable, manipulating Castaneda, who is always over-heating, always vulnerable, constantly having to face his own panic.

As an image of the 'impeccable shaman,' Castaneda's don Juan has contributed much to the seductive glamour of the shamanic revival. To be impeccable means to be faultless. But we need to ask to what extent has this popular image of shamanic invulnerability — of 'the shaman with the perfect energy body' — fed our rootless narcissism, intent upon looking cool and manipulating others? Do these grandiose images compensate, perhaps, for an experience of disempowerment in our everyday lives? Does the image of the impeccable shaman help us to face this sense of powerlessness? Does it nurture that gentle dedication, Hillman's 'faithful attention,' to the more subtle, but intimately accessible stirrings of our own psyche, as it opens up to an awareness of the living presences, or spirits, within and around us?

The shamanic quest is an expression of the need to reclaim a lost spiritual dimension in our lives. But despite a genuine desire to reconnect with spirit, we may clothe our aspirations in images and practices which lead to a dead-end. Instead of becoming a means of living life more deeply — grounded and at home on Earth — these images and practices shoot the individual off into the far reaches of inner space. The spiritual, or rather — more accurately — the 'astral' worlds, and everyday life, become two distinct, often incompatible, domains. Instead of becoming more integrated, a person may be torn apart. For along with that genuine desire to embrace life, lies another powerful urge — its shadow side — of wanting to escape from life, from its stressful, abrasive, constricting mundanity into some other magical realm, where the universe, it is hoped, will cater for one's every whim.

James Hillman is not only wary of aspirations like don Juan's, to fly off into infinity, to dissolve or lift off, he is also sharply critical of all forms of spirituality which involve this need for absolute transcendence, seeing them as a threat to the values of 'soul.'

> I think that the spiritual disciplines are part of the disaster of the world. They forsake the world to its pollution, to its toxicity, to its corruption.
> I think it's an absolute horror that someone could be so filled with what the Greeks called *superbia*, to think that his personal, little, tiny self-transcendence is more important than the world and the beauty of the world: the trees, the animals, the people, the buildings, the culture. What is the psychological pull of this transcendence? What is happening in the psyche that could make a person so incredibly self-centered? So self-centered to say, "Good-bye brothers, good-bye children, good-bye wife, good-bye flowers, good-bye everything. I'm off to the snowy heights. I want an imageless white liberation and freedom from the cycle of birth and rebirth."[15]

Do the teachings of don Juan help us to embrace life, or do they present an image of withdrawal from it into a colorful but isolated metaphysical realm? Their appeal lies primarily in their promise of power, freedom, and an escape into a world that bears little relationship to our own day-to-day experience. Nor is don Juan's universe fully 'shamanic' in that it lacks one vital ingredient of shamanism—the tribe. He believes that there are no social functions for modern shamans as there were in the past. He himself is portrayed by Castaneda as possessing the psychic powers of the shaman, and the shaman's ability to be an intermediate between the seen and the unseen worlds. But in his goal to blast off, to transcend the world and navigate the infinite, does he have the healing heart—the soul or spirit—of the shaman?

Tribal reservations and grounds for doubt
Castaneda has said that, 'One needs a lifetime to acquire

membership in a cultural world,' and after more than thirty years of involvement with the shamans of ancient Mexico he did not feel he belonged to that world sufficiently to draw conclusions about it. Despite his tendency to be enigmatic and to mystify shamanism, Castaneda is highlighting here a genuine, basic problem that anthropologists have to face when studying the spiritual life of tribal peoples. For a sacred tribal event, like a ritual, is no longer sacred when performed for an outsider. The very essence of ritual activity is that it creates a setting in which the unexpected may occur. The ritual is the stage upon which the spontaneous expressions of the tribal spirits are enacted. The sacred itself is beyond words, an area which can only be experienced within that culture. In this sense, the spiritual life of tribal peoples cannot be communicated to those outside the tribe, and the traditional forms which are shown to outsiders are bound to be secular imitations of the sacred. They are predictable and generally do not vary; rather than being enactments of the sacred, they are acts which have been 'packaged' for outsiders, lacking the inspiration of the unexpected, and the meaning of the moment in which they occurred.

An outsider can only take away a pale imitation of the sacred from tribal life, its external trappings, cut off from its spiritual meaning and cultural roots. For the meaning and purpose of a sacred, tribal ritual is not only tied to the moment of its enactment, it is also grounded in the spirits of the *place* in which tribal peoples live. Spirits not only permeate the life of tribal societies, they also inhabit distinct locations on tribal lands, and these spirits of place may often be bound up with deep resonances from the past—with the tribal ancestors.

If the full meaning of tribal spirituality cannot be experienced by an outsider, how can it be transplanted to another, non-tribal culture? Anthropologist Michael Harner has been very much a driving force behind the active revival of shamanic practices in the West, with the spread of his popular 'core' shamanic workshops. By attending these workshops, people learn to journey, to contact their power animals, and even to carry out soul retrievals.

Harner is a man with a mission, with a sense of urgency to help save the world. His neo-shamanism offers instant access to the world of 'the spirits' for individuals in our highly mobile, spiritually confused culture. But it does little to prepare the *cultural ground* for a collective shamanic awakening. Modern culture is neither tribal nor animistic in outlook. An enormous gulf exists between the native communities, in which shamanism does have a place, and our Western culture. Not only do tribal peoples usually have the animistic view of the universe, they also have a more social sense of the self than we do—a self more embedded within the community. This is the shamanic world in which the life of the community and the activity of the shaman are entwined, both permeated with a belief in spirits. It is this fact—that tribal peoples organize their lives around sacred shamanic tasks—which enables their practices to take place with complete integrity. In our culture we do not have these tasks, this organization, or integrity.

Having researched shamanism in tribal cultures, and witnessed from its outset the shamanic revival in the West, Joan Halifax has also expressed her own reservations about it.

> ...one of my reservations about shamanism has been that the psychological, philosophical, and ethical elaborations which would make shamanism relevant to people today do not exist in an accessible way for the most part. Tribal shamanism is appropriate for people living in tribal societies; but those who live in modern Western society would seem to need something generated from its own social ground.[16]

In order to be effective, the tribal shaman often depends upon the support of the tribe, upon its energy, to help propel him or her into the world of the spirits. For example, amongst the Eskimos described by Knud Rasmussen, a shaman might need to boost his self-confidence by denigrating his own shamanic abilities in front of the group which has assembled for a ritual. The group would then hail him as a great shaman and urge him to go on with the ritual. In this way, the shaman would be able to focus his energies, having drawn on the tribe's firm belief, both in him and in a world of spirits. In the absence of this supportive, social dimension to the shamanic quest, without the collective energy of the community to back up our journeys, we are left questioning the meaning and purpose of reviving traditional shamanic practices in the West. There may be a great thrill in having one's inner world burst into life through the beating of a drum during the shamanic journey. But apart from this, the question which arises over and over again is, 'How does all this relate to my everyday life, to the world I live in today?' This problem of relevance is something observed frequently by Jonathan Horwitz, director of the Scandinavian Center for Shamanic Studies.

> ...many people have a problem bringing the results of their shamanic and/or other spiritual work into everyday life, and as a result, drift away from it, remembering in the back of their consciousness that they have those connections but do not use them. I think we've all experienced this at one stage or another, if not most of the time.[17]

Our culture is highly intellectual and analytical in orientation. It is a predominantly 'left-brain' culture. Pretending to go native through the drumming, rattling, and journeying of the shamanic workshop may temporarily suppress our dominant left-brain consciousness, but it will still be there when we go back home, or start work again on Monday morning.

The packaged rituals and practices of neo-shamanism also bypass the often long, arduous, and solitary path of shamanic initiation, literally 'storming' the Western psyche, especially through drumming and journeying. These activities can have an enormously liberating effect upon people, especially if their lives have been hidebound by conformity, self-consciousness and an over-dependency upon intellect. But this feeling of liberation often takes place within a cultural vacuum, so that the psychic life of a person pursuing neo-shamanism fails to find expression within its own social ground. Perhaps it does not matter that the practices of neo-shamanism are largely irrelevant to everyday life. Perhaps it is the experience of liberation, and a taste of the shamanic universe, that provides adequate reason to engage in them. But there is a further problem with the neo-shamanic agenda, which is more serious, as it may lead to states of psychological disorientation and disintegration, rather than deeper psychospiritual integration. This is the often unacknowledged danger of an individual being sucked back into atavistic energies and resonances of past times.

The pull of the past

Like Michael Harner, many of us have seen the world on the brink of destruction, and sense a sometimes desperate need for an awakening, both in ourselves and in society as a whole. We experience a deep desire to heal the world, to become more integrated within ourselves, and to re-harmonize our imbalanced relationship with the natural world. But we lack the earth-rooted spiritual ground in our own culture through which this awakening can take place. So we look back through time to peoples whose spirituality has survived from ancient times.

No doubt many Western spiritual seekers have had 'past lives' as shamans, or as members of shamanic communities. There may be a genuine, deep, inner pull towards shamanism, not simply for its value as a path to spiritual awakening, but towards the actual energies which have been generated by shamanic ritual in the past. They experience a deep memory, of a time when their lives were more tribal, both more communal and also more finely attuned to the rhythms and cycles of the natural world. So they look to the practices of tribal peoples today to help them evoke that memory. But as with any past-life scenario, shamanism needs to be approached for what it can offer to the here-and-now, to the culture of today. And unless they take the greatest of care, a person may be subtly, but inexorably, drawn back into energies of the past, which were appropriate then, but which may not be so helpful to them now. When confronted with my own dilemma of this ancient shamanic memory, pulling me away from the demands of everyday life, I sought guidance from Gildas, the discarnate wise guide, channeled by Ruth White.

From Gildas's perspective, there *is* a place in our culture today for ancient approaches to spirituality like shamanism. But he has also given a very clear teaching, and a stern warning, about the way in which we approach them.

> The question outlines a certain area which it is necessary to be aware of. This is the area of looking into the past, to times when rituals and ways of living were appropriate, and then assuming that those things are entirely appropriate to bring forward, as they were known then, into the present...This is very rarely so. It is not easy to bring something forward from the past in terms of your linear time. It is especially not easy to bring something forward from the past across lines of culture.[18]

Gildas points out that the evocation of a certain kind of memory is important today. This is the memory of the power and the meaning of the rituals through which tribal cultures have attuned to the world of spirit in the past. It is this 're-membering' which may help us reconnect with Earth's spirit. But it is the way in which this memory is evoked, and the way in which it is then used, which Gildas believes needs special attention.

> The memory which comes more from the intellect, from intellectual research, and then from an attunement, an opening, or a sense of recognition, is not sufficient. The memory which has to be opened is the memory which comes more deeply from the instinct, from the instinctual and the intuitional level.

In the last chapter, we saw how the experience of solitude on the shamanic path might lead to contact with this deep instinctual level of our being. But this inner exploration also requires the suspension of intellect to enable the living energies from the elemental worlds to enter consciousness. Gildas, too, warns that the deep memory of our more instinctual tribal past cannot be evoked through the intellect alone, and that we need to reawaken another faculty which long ago went into disuse.

> That memory cannot come until there has been more work done on the opening of the alter major chakra. This is the chakra which is situated in the head, near the bottom of the skull. This is where the main energy point of that chakra is in terms of the physical body. It is the chakra which, when opened, allows the racial and the collective memory to be incorporated into the time in which you live. But it is incorporated in such a way that it is brought forward in a form and in an expression that is suitable for the times and for that culture. This applies to memory within a culture and to memory which goes across cultures.

As we saw in Chapter 3, this alter major chakra awareness underlies the origins of shamanism thousands of years ago amongst our Paleolithic ancestors in ice-age Europe. It is an instinctual level of awareness which later became eclipsed, as consciousness contracted and the self-consciousness of intellect became the dominant cognitive tool which we modern humans use to negotiate our reality.

It is no use our pretending today either that we still possess an opened 'alter major' awareness which allows us to attune naturally to the past, or that in the course of a week-end shamanic workshop we can override thousands of years of evolving human consciousness. Regaining that ancient, instinctual awareness is bound to be a gradual process—of loosening and moving beyond the sharp edge of intellect.

> I am concerned, many are concerned on this side of life—and indeed on your side of life—about the entry into this recognition from the direction of the intellect. The information is then used in order to try to simulate the experience and, through that experience, the memory is sought to be enhanced. This is what might be termed *a retrograde step*.

When we try to simulate the experience of past practices and rituals, there is the real danger that these rituals, possessing a resonance and autonomy of their own, will draw individuals and groups into acting them out unconsciously. As Gildas points out, '...forces are released which can no longer be managed. Deep things are released from levels which have been allowed to become unconscious, and which have not come forward in consciousness in an organic way.' We might get 'sucked back' into an atavistic and unconscious acting out of energies which simply do not belong to where we are today.

A ritual, and the level of consciousness which it expresses, is very much married to a time and a place, and to the needs of the people in that culture. But life and consciousness are always evolving.

> So much has moved on, so much has changed. Those rituals are inappropriate in that form. The essence of the ritual is not inappropriate, but it does depend on the direction from which the attunement to it is coming. When the attunement is natural, then the ritual will automatically live and be changed. When the attunement is more intellectual, then it will have to be brought forward as near as possible in its once-known form. This means that those who take part in those rituals, brought forward in this way, are not prepared for the experiences which will be evoked by the ritual.
>
> So approach these things with care and with consciousness.

Gildas's message of caution provides an important perspective over a difficult terrain. A New Age movement like neo-shamanism is brought into being by a genuine, urgent desire in people for healing and wholeness, to marry instinct and intellect, and to find a more vital experience of being alive. But its flip side, or shadow, is an often equally pressing need to escape from life. Faced with the uncertainty of modern life and the confusion of a rapidly transforming world, we may become mesmerized by the past, and seduced into believing that it contains the answers to our future. But as Tad Mann observes in his book, *Millennium Prophesies*, 'No-one seems able to imagine what our future will be like, because we are looking to the past for our answers.'[19] Perhaps the New Age shaman will be not so much involved in reviving shamanic practices of the past as in being the animating force behind a new vision for the future.

CHAPTER 8

THE QUEST FOR POWER

Knowledge must be burned, hammered and beaten like pure gold. Then one can wear it as an ornament.
Tibetan saying

In exploring this vast field of human experience, which we call 'shamanism,' I have attempted to draw as clear an outline as possible of who and what a shaman is. But in seeking to define the shaman, we need to remember that this is essentially an exercise which helps *us* to talk about the experiences and practices of this tribal person whom *we* call a 'shaman.' The word itself would mean little or nothing to the vast majority of those individuals who, over the aeons of our evolution, have kept the flame of the human spirit burning through their ability and willingness to propel themselves beyond the confines of everyday consciousness on behalf of their tribe. Attempting to define a shaman is bound to omit, distort or misrepresent much of that largely ineffable body of human experience which we now label as 'shamanism.'

The word *shaman* was adopted by anthropologists from the Tungus tribe in Siberia. It was then used by academics as a general term to be able to talk about the practices of these specially gifted individuals in tribal societies worldwide. It became an '-ism' — shamanism — so that these experiences and practices could be neatly accommodated by the Western intellectual mind. But shamanic experience cannot be approached through the intellect alone. It is like trying to understand a live snake by chopping off its head.

Coleridge once said, 'We murder to dissect,' and the sharp edge of the Western analytical mind often destroys the object of its curiosity — whatever it considers strange, exotic, or 'other' — without truly entering into the experience and reality of that 'other.' Laurens van der Post saw this in the attitude of scientists towards the Bushmen of the Kalihari, whom he loved, and whose mind and spirit he was able to interpret more deeply and intimately than perhaps any other Western writer. In his book, *The Heart of the Hunter*, he describes how scientists often begged to come with him on his visits to the Kalihari.

> ....because they wanted to measure Bushman heads and behinds, others to measure his sexual organs, others to study his family relationships, and one to analyze his spit; but when I asked them if they were not interested in the Bushman's mind and spirit, in the man as a living whole, they replied: 'That is not our department of science.' We seemed to have destroyed the Bushman without ever bothering to find out what sort of person he really was.[1]

Once shamanism had become an academic subject, dissected into its essential components by historians and anthropologists, the next step would be to repackage these core ingredients as 'neo-shamanism,' more amenable to the growing numbers of people in the New Age movement seeking self-empowerment and inner transformation during the late 20th and early 21st centuries.

Our world is crying out for the collective awakening of our indigenous spirit—the spirit of shamanism—as part of a wider, deeper New Age transformation of consciousness. But this transformation is essentially an inner process. As David Spangler has pointed out, New Age spirituality does not need to be shown off dramatically in a flamboyant or sensational manner. Inner change may simply result in a letting go of fear, so that we feel lighter, things happen for us more gracefully, we might become 'less pressured, kinder, gentler.' We become more whole.

Clearly, for some people, coming into contact with the energies of the shamanic archetype may animate and transform their lives in a simple and graceful way. Others, by contrast, may identify with these energies, giving rise to an inflation rather than a transformation of self. This is a particular hazard for people who see themselves as shamans in our own non-tribal society, where we no longer have the spiritual or cultural traditions of shamanism to support the role.

Awakening to the spirit of shamanism does not mean becoming invulnerable and all-powerful, as the Castaneda-inspired cult-image of the shaman suggests. Rather, it implies acknowledging our wounds, going into them, facing up to a sense of powerlessness, and seeing our vulnerabilities as a source of strength rather than as a weakness. For it is through knowing and accepting ourselves just as we are — both the positive and the negative — that a point of inner equilibrium may be found. Once we become grounded in that essential, secure, balanced center, we may then be able to open up to a deeper experience of life, and perhaps a lighter, more transcending, and expanded sense of ourselves.

Without that self-acceptance and without that balance, we go on denying our negative feelings and fail to understand why we need them. We start to look outside for images of power which will compensate for these denials, and through which we can buy a feeling of strength and empowerment. Elements of the 'spiritual supermarket' within the neo-shamanic movement cater for this need, proffering power as a kind of quick spiritual fix, obscuring the true calling of the shaman, and leading to the posturing of a vapid, self-centered pseudo-shamanism.

The problem of power

I've heard enough of 'power.' Power animals, power dances, power lunches. We have allowed our society to make us feel so small and out of control that we are eager clients for anything selling the concept of power. We clothe our quest in its images.[2]

The Tungus shaman speaking here, Mika Amuru, goes on to make a plea for 'connection, relation, vision,' to counter the excessive marketing of power which is common in contemporary neo-shamanism. There, the grandiose image of the shaman as an impeccable, modern hero-savior is often promoted and associated with the promise of self-empowerment. Mika Amuru's plea is not to attach so much glamor to the person of the shaman who is 'a go-between, a tool, not an ascended master.' He reminds us that a shaman may be no more spiritually developed than anyone else.

> The shaman in this world is like all of us — frail or strong, good of heart or petty, truthful or deceitful. S/he simply has the propensity for trance, which when properly trained allows access to the Worlds.[3]

While Mika Amuru stresses the shaman's ordinariness in order to offset the tendency to elevate them, both spiritually and morally, Gildas, by contrast, emphasizes the shaman's sense of calling and dedication to their path. He does so in order to counterbalance the expectation that shamanic practices will provide us with quick, magical solutions to our problems.

> Although everyone can have an inner relationship with shamanism, it's just not appropriate that there should be so many practicing this neo-shamanism without the realization of the dedication and the true calling which goes with it.
> Of course it's seductive — all want to be chosen, all want to journey....Sometimes shamanism can seem an easy or magical way, a spectacular way. But it's also a very dedicated and sacred way.[4]

The path towards becoming a shaman in tribal cultures is often a hard path, entailing deprivation and suffering, or at least solitude, before the shaman is ready to serve the community. The quick fix offered by many a neo-shamanic workshop could be seen to trivialize this traditional, sacred path. Its storming of the psyche to gain instant access to the worlds of spirit is in stark contrast to the often long, intimate path of inner searching, which many traditional shamans have to go through. Each individual, whether tribal or Western, needs to follow their own inner promptings and to awaken to spirit in their own time, in their own way, at the rhythm and tempo which suits them — not in response to the strident call to

'Wake up now, or sleep forever.' This fearful threat of global doom and destruction underlies the marketing of a number of New Age techniques for spiritual awakening, including core shamanism.

Awakening to the spirit of shamanism, to the expanded awareness of our more instinctual spirituality, is an inner process. Proponents of neo-shamanism present it from outside by preaching the shamanic world-view and by marketing tribal rituals and practices. As an evangelical movement, the goal is to spread the word as quickly as possible, so that the distilled practices of the tribal shaman are fed to sometimes large groups of people. When many people undertake journeys—and even soul retrievals—at the same time under the same roof, there is great scope for mental, emotional, and spiritual confusion. Individuals may get their psychic wires crossed, and delusional information may be transmitted from 'the spirits' in non-ordinary reality. As Gildas has said, 'It was never meant that crowds of people should practice shamanism,'[5] and in their haste to awaken the world, those who mass-market neo-shamanism may, perhaps unwittingly, be inducing a bigger sleep.

The practices of neo-shamanism are not designed to develop consciousness, self-awareness, or compassion. Rather, they tend in the opposite direction—towards reduced consciousness and minimal self-reflection. This is a large part of their appeal—to engage in a form of selective dissociation, or trance. Our problems and decisions are handed over to the spirits during the shamanic journey, and if one is lucky, then a higher dimension or level of wisdom will be contacted to help us with these problems. But equally, a lower and mischievous level of consciousness may be contacted; and because people receive advice on their journeys—because messages come during visions—this advice or these messages are commonly treated as coming from a higher authority than our own reasoning and everyday common sense. And there is tremendous scope here for a subtle abuse of power, for I can parade my message 'from the spirits' as possessing a certain moral authority, but at the time exempt myself from any responsibility for the content or consequences of it, since it came from '*the* spirits.'

All forms of spirituality, both past and present, including neo-shamanism, fall prey to this equation in which being psychic and having visions is confused with being spiritual or wise. Neo-shamanism is promoted as a path to self-empowerment. But without the spiritual and social foundations of tribal societies, this blend of past and present, of tribal and non-tribal cultures, can result in an indigestible stew of psychospiritual confusion, ego inflation, the violation of psychological boundaries, and the abuse of personal power. As Gildas has pointed out, 'Where there are those who come into shamanism because of a need to find a spectacular and flamboyant power, then there will always be the power struggle.'[6]

While Mircea Eliade defined shamanism as 'archaic techniques of ecstasy,' emphasizing the shaman's magical flight into the spirit world, Castaneda glamorized the shaman's power, impeccability, and transcendent individualism. Together these have made up a very seductive image through which to sell neo-shamanism to a large number of people. But as an actual experience it needs to be tempered with well-grounded discernment, balance, and a sense of perspective.

Twenty-first century spirit

With the increasing popularity of neo-shamanism, the shamanic journey has become a consumer item. As such it may be the fashionable thing to have or to do at the moment. But like many consumer items, we often forget to ask 'Do we really need it?' For as English-born Lama and Tantric shaman, Ngakpa Chögyam Rinpoche points out, 'There's absolutely no point in teaching people to conjure with intangible worlds when their conventional, tangible world is a total mess.'[7]

My own feeling is that, in the 21st century, we have arrived at a point in our evolution where we no longer necessarily have to rely upon elaborate rituals and ceremonies from the past, or heavy astral psychism, to see or move into 'the worlds beyond.' Advances in our understanding of the universe from modern physics have already indicated that spirit, matter, and consciousness are all forms of energy. Matter is seen as condensed spirit, a denser form of energy on a slower rate of vibration than many other levels of spirit, but it is a spiritual energy all the same. The material world is seen as but one of the myriad of interpenetrating realms of existence or dimensions of experience within an unbounded spiritual universe. From this perspective, the physical world we see, hear, touch, smell, or taste *is* the world beyond, only perceived strangely through the senses. We do not have to propel ourselves out of the physical body and soar away from Earth in order to sense the centering warmth of our own eternal, living flame, or spirit. It is right here.

Ken Carey's beautiful transmissions of wisdom, *Starseed The Third Millennium*, puts out the same message.

> There is but the finest veil between you and a full-dimensional perception of reality, the filmiest of screens between you and your eternal self. You require no elaborate technique or ritual to release this veil. You need only open to the organic current of awareness that in every moment flows to you from the source of life.[8]

The wisdom and energy emanating from these finer frequencies of awareness and intelligence are already creating a new vision, a new myth, the essential rainbow bridge, which the human tribe needs to cross in order to open its heart, expand its awareness, and experience that 'organic current of awareness' flowing into it.

The vision of shamanism presented in Part III of this book also emanates from a more finely-tuned state of consciousness than the more time-bound awareness of normal, everyday life. It has been channeled from a level of clear consciousness, a location of spirit, where many lifetimes of shamanic experience have been integrated and condensed. As the final part of this book's panoramic view over the vast field of shamanism, it is very much a vision of the future. While we cannot go back to the primal mind of our ancestors, we can reclaim that lost awareness, and integrate it into a deeper experience and understanding of who—on Earth—we are today, and where we might be going.

The shaman has become a potent symbol of our mystic participation with Earth's spirit. But we do not all have to follow the dedicated path and enact the specialist role of the traditional, tribal shaman in order to regain this primal awareness. What was once the sole preserve of the shaman in tribal societies, or of the mystic in the West, is now an embryonic, collective awareness of that essential, elemental force which animates every cell in the body of every human being incarnate on the planet. It is our awakening to the spirit of shamanism.

PART III

THE SPIRIT OF SHAMANISM

CHAPTER 9

AT HOME ON EARTH

The spirit of shamanism brings from the ancient past into your present life the light of experience, as part of the dawning of a new consciousness. It brings resonance and depth, so that in your life you may know that you belong to the body of humanity and to the body of this Earth.

Pathways run to and fro, from memories which are so deeply embedded in the story of humankind. There can be no reconciliation with where you are now until you allow that natural spirit, which you call shamanism, to be physically embodied in the life of the modern human tribe. What you think of as shamanism is much less an idea, than the awareness of all the relationships which you bring to bear when you incarnate physically — the root, the stem, the branches, the leaves, the flowers, the tree of life. These are not symbols but the manifestation and expression of the serpent current of life. The primal mind today sleeps but cries out in a fitful dream, as if half aware of what is going on in your so-called 'wakefulness.' Unanswered questions will remain unanswered until you are prepared to let go and let flow that little stream of your personal consciousness and know it to be a moment's blinking of sunlight on the wave of the greater stream. Your consciousness is in no way separate, only highlighted temporarily, caught in the act of seeing itself reflected by light.

The integrated shaman
I can hear the question coming now of where this level of awareness is, of whose consciousness this is. This is that point of integrated consciousness where the many living echoes of shamanic incarnations enter into the present life of this shaman-sensitive. He has wanted to deny his shamanic lives in many ways, because of the pain experienced during them, which was re-

awoken and became apparent. Through these communications there may be a much greater acceptance of that elemental spirit which has been embodied in those many lives. In denying the pain, he was trying to deny the whole spirit. But when the pain is faced, the spirit may once again begin to be embodied.

This is the deep, living memory of the many times when the spirit of Earth has been embraced. And there is so much more coming for the human race in its relationship with Earth. There is a much greater unfolding to be allowed and enabled, in fuller consciousness — a true awakening.

In the past, in your past, the shaman has been one who serves, one who puts their own sense of self in the community to the side, so that they may be there for the tribe. And there was often a sorrow from having to pass by what was normal for most people, in order to be of service. Today this is not necessary. To be a shaman today does not mean — or does not need to mean — to be outside or beyond the tribe. To be a shaman today requires being fully integrated within it. There have always been degrees of integration or dis-integration in the shaman's relationship to the tribe. But the call today is greater than ever not to stay outside of society, not to remain on the edges, but to be fully integrated in whatever way, and then bring to bear that spirit of shamanism upon the life of the tribe.

Today, more than ever before, the role of the shaman is to help each person to remember that they belong to each other; and not only to each other, but to the land, the stones, the trees, the rivers, the sky. The spirits of places need to be recognized and reawakened in human consciousness. The new spirits of places which are forming — the spirits in the world which has been constructed — need to be acknowledged and recognized. The world needs to be remembered as alive in all its manifestations.

The roots of every place go down through the elements. The foundations are laid in the elements. This elemental awareness is what the spirit of shamanism is about. The metals out of which modern life is built, the deep, dark energies of the plastics, the oils, and the chemicals, all need to be acknowledged and awakened as spirit. The world needs to be redeemed as spirit and known as possessing soul, for it is soul which embodies spirit, it is spirit which animates soul.

A sense of belonging

The spirit of shamanism is the living energy of that deep sense of belonging and participation, which the spirit of humanity has at its foundation with the spirit of planet Earth. It is there for all, not just the select or gifted few. It is there whether a person perceives it or not. There could be no life on this planet without constant, ongoing sharing and participation between all forms of life. You may think that there has been a dislocation within your mind, so that you cannot feel that living spirit flowing through and between every form of creation. But there could be no life without it.

A sense of belonging is your birthright; and instead of taking up your birthright, you had to create artificial structures, hierarchies which give you a false sense of belonging. Instead of belonging to Earth, which is your very first and most essential community, you have created human structures where you feel comforted by being dominated by others. You have placed yourself under authorities that divest you of the courage and of that vital edge which enable you to stand on Earth and sense your true kinship with this wider, deeper, awesome Being. You have substituted distorted notions of power for the true numinous power of your own incarnation.

You have a choice, whether to experience this sense of belonging, or whether to continue to be denigrated by the history and patterns of civilizations, which have imposed a crippling sense of worthlessness upon the majority of human beings, often in the name of false gods. How can you belong to Earth when you are made to feel worthless, when the words that you use to denigrate each other are often the names of animals which co-habit Earth with you?

The spirit of belonging brings with it certain qualities—of respect as opposed to cynicism, of honoring your life as opposed to criticizing and devaluing it, of allowing yourself to tread more lightly upon Earth instead of blundering, smashing, cutting and damaging. The experience of belonging to Earth will become more and more amenable than it has been in the past, for the conditions are riper for it now. The forces that have sabotaged this experience are being contained, so that you may drink more fully of your life on Earth and know why you are here.

The question of why you are here does not need to arise if you are able to meet and greet all the other forms of life around you, and allow yourself to be met and greeted by them. When you feel you are known and recognized in this way, you do not become so obsessed by human life and culture. The Bushman, for example, knew the universe he inhabited, and felt known by it. But this way of being has been lost in the modern era. So the task lies ahead of trying to recognize the universe which you inhabit, and of allowing yourselves to be recognized by it, so that it can speak to you.

Reanimating the miscreated

If you allow it, the spirit of shamanism can really animate the world in which you live. As it awakens within you, this spirit will enable you to engage not simply with natural forms, but with all forms, whether they are natural creations or human constructions. As you learn to feel this spirit more consciously, within your own physical being, and to sense your belonging to Earth, you will be able to engage with all the materials which are in use within your culture, no matter how artificial, toxic, polluted, or unnatural they may seem. It will be possible, in a sense, to reanimate the 'miscreated.' For once something has been created, it cannot be uncreated. So many modern materials are made out of the residue of millions and millions of years of growth and decay on this planet. The oils you use for fuel and the petrochemicals which make plastics, for example, belong to a time when humanity had yet to manifest fully upon Earth. In a sense, the use of these ancient residues for the manufacture of these materials makes the task deeper and even more sacred—to acknowledge them as being imbued with spirit. At the same time, you need to be aware of their compatibility with the functioning of your own physical bodies. For human life on Earth is very delicate, and there are many conditions upon and within this planet which are not compatible with human life—which have their own purpose.

The oils which have been extracted from Earth should really have remained in their own domain, for they are not compatible with human physical life. They belong to another cycle and stream of evolution which has taken place on this planet. Your use of these residues, in a sense, violates certain laws of Earth's being. But since that violation has taken place, it needs to be accommodated and contained, and these materials need to be acknowledged as an expression of spirit, for they *are* an expression of spirit, even if they have their own domain.

Many of the chemicals which have been conjured up by technology also urgently need to be acknowledged as spirit. Like oil-derived products, they need to be contained, as many of them endanger life on Earth. They are expressions of elemental worlds which have been distorted through the need and greed of humankind; as such they represent a violation of your relationship with these kingdoms. This is one reason why a renewed sense of belonging to Earth is so important. Respectful cohabitation with these kingdoms would ensure that this violation does not occur again.

With a deeper sense of belonging to Earth, its abuse could not take place, because people would understand that the gift of consciousness permeates all kingdoms, and is not their sole prerogative. The clatter of intellect has become so loud that it has deafened itself to the whispering from other kingdoms in the natural world. For example, the minerals—at the best of times—have a deep, deep, gentle and quiet voice, as far as human perception is concerned. With all your mental noise, a balanced relationship has become impossible. The sense of belonging and relating to the rest of life on Earth is really going to depend upon a quietening, rebalancing, and reorientation of the human mind.

The monumental task

In your tribal past, the community was the total life of the individual. If a person was cast out of the tribe, this often entailed a loss of their sense of self. They became a ghost to others, and therefore to themselves. They were hardly visible, and this for them was real. This was a time when 'I' and the tribe were very close, and the individual belonged to the larger body — the larger body defined the individual. Today it is through the larger bodies of the whole of humanity, and of that great being — Earth — that you need to define yourself whilst on Earth. There needs to be a true expansion of that fragmented particle of awareness back out into the total field of your being and experience. It is as if the whole of Western culture expelled itself from the body of Earth, and also from its own body of humanity. It is as if you became ghosts to yourselves, and now you need to work *so hard* to create a sense of self, an identity, to assert your individuality within the void of your ghost-like expulsion.

But when you remember — and not just as an intellectual exercise — but when you truly remember, when you experience your own body as the root, the stem and the flower — as an expression of Earth — then there will be no need for all those massive, monumental endeavors, which you currently strive to achieve in order to momentarily generate a sense of self, an identity for yourself. Life on Earth, and life in general — not necessarily just on Earth — guarantees your identity. Your belonging, and who you are, are guaranteed. The ease with which this is forgotten is part of an overall pattern of growing more fully into consciousness of your deeper spiritual being — this forgetting and remembering again. But the forgetting has become stuck in time, and it needs to be remembered again, in time. It is as if the pendulum which swings with the rhythms of the natural cycles became stuck and held in one position, at an extreme. But in these days, that tension of holding the rhythm out of balance can be released slowly, gently, so that you may stand at the central point. So long as you try to hold your consciousness at that point of extreme self-consciousness, of consciousness only of the individual fragment, you will always find the way to that sense of belonging closed to you. The energy needs to be released from this monumental task of maintaining your separate self. That sense of your own uniqueness will not disappear with the regained experience of belonging, as you fear it may. You have to work so hard to maintain that position that you are left drained and exhausted. If you just open out, breathe out your self, there is nothing to lose.

A world beyond words

When you truly regain your sense of belonging to Earth, this elemental awareness automatically brings with it a gentleness and humility towards all other expressions of life. When this sense of belonging is fully experienced, there can be none of the arrogance that characterizes the Western mind still today, the arrogance of the superiority of intellect. And while this may be a book about shamanism, it simply cannot teach more than a minute fraction of what can be experienced, learned, and understood through that greater openness towards the messages in the sky, in the clouds, in the whispering of the winds, in every utterance coming from each manifestation of life around you. When you allow your eyes to see and your ears to hear, you will wonder how you could have relied so much and for so long on the words written in books. This is not to devalue the writing of books, for through them you might find a path to this expanded awareness. But it is important to remember here that words can sometimes disguise the universe of experience which lies behind and beyond them; and it is towards this whole ineffable world of broader, deeper experience that this book is pointing.

CHAPTER 10

WHOLEHEARTED INCARNATION

You lift one pearl and present it as a gift. Here, from where we see the endless transformations of personal history, there is a true sense of opportunity now to bring a total synthesis of those many distinct yet unified experiences as the shaman. Those incarnations may once have seemed like burdens carried on the shoulders. But now they can be laid to rest, even while their energetic essence remains. The tension held through the need to balance the positive with the negative may now be experienced more as the warm flow and pulse of the blood through the veins, as a physical balancing, as rhythmic, physical life.

The idea of engaging consciously, in a wholehearted manner, with the elemental qualities through which life expresses itself on planet Earth can become a living experience. It is not simply an idea, but thought made manifest, starting at the point of physical incarnation. For that is the focus of each individual. Too often the structures and belief systems of the world have coerced the soul and the spirit away from full expression in the body. They have made it seem as if there is no fertile soil in which to plant the seed of consciousness at the deeply physical level. Many people have experienced this, especially those who are sensitive to what seems like an overwhelming pull away from the planet. For them it is as if 'going home' is somewhere far away from Earth. But while Earth may be only one of many forms of life and experience in the universe, your 'home' may be experienced at the same time in any or all of these places. It is truly hologrammic, in the sense that the center is everywhere at once, not in some distant heaven. No matter where you are, you carry that center in all times and in all places.

The song of incarnation
The spirit of shamanism is an aspect of Earth's spirit. It is that vibrant, living pulse which animates every expression of life, and courses through your veins. And if you were just to stop for one moment to reflect, and to enter into your own skin, and feel your own heartbeat, that heartbeat is the constant reminder, while you are alive on Earth, that you belong to Earth. It is the constant reminder of who you are, for it is the beat of your own soul, and the beat of your soul is animated by your own unique spirit.

This essential experience has been overlaid by all the theories and distortions of the scientific mind, which tries to explain away your vibrant, essential experience of being alive. It tries to tell you what the heart is, and that the soul does not exist, nor the spirit. But in that very immediate pulsing, you have your identity. In that rhythm, in each and every throb, you can sense and know that you belong to Earth. That gentle moment to pause, reflect, and feel, is an instant reminder of who you are and that you belong here to Earth. The heartbeat is the song of physical incarnation on Earth, and the breath, the rhythm of the breath, is the expression of your spirit.

In many ways, this is such a simple experience. But it has become complicated, distorted, and narrowed by the multitudes of thoughts and ideas, which overlay and suffocate the experience of life. So just let the sky clear. Let the dust—those particles of thought—settle. In a sense, these many, many ideas are polluting your clear perception. The impulse behind science is a wonderful sense of curiosity and play. It is a spirited undertaking. But science has set out from a point which can lead nowhere, before the act of remembering has taken place. It is curiosity blindfolded. It is a playful endeavor, but playful as if a child were asked to dance with shackles around its legs. And the endless theories are spawned in a kind of desperation to seek the truth, which is so much closer than can be known through the methods of science as they are today.

It is not only the mind of science which is looking through a thick pane of glass at the vibrant living world. For science is simply the institutionalization of the Western mind. It is the communal Western mind floundering, reaching beyond itself to discover something which is within. Science must move towards a deeper knowing, a knowing which comes from that sense of belonging, not from trying to be the detached observer. There is no such thing as a detached observer in the whole universe. You may still your mind, to be a more *quiet* observer of experience. But detachment is a self-imposed illusion which has become reality, so that your detachment means that you no longer see, hear, or sense life within and around you.

The power animal and incarnation

Traditionally, the shaman has been helped by their power animal, and today, more and more people in the West are finding help through contact with their elemental spirit helpers, or animal 'allies.' But whether the person is a tribal shaman, or a Western shaman, or simply someone who wishes to reconnect with the spirit of shamanism, again, as you move into the future, there can be a new understanding of this essential relationship. For the power animal may be understood as *Earth's energy configuring itself for the individual*. It is Earth's spirit taking on a form and entering your awareness, so that you may relate to it personally. Everyone always has this elemental energy within and around them, whatever they may call it. It is always there, but in the modern, 'developed' world, it has been forgotten.

The power animal is the configuration of Earth's spirit through which you can fully experience yourself as belonging totally — for the time you are here — to this planet, so that it is truly your home. It is 'you' as if you were not so much 'simply human', as *a whole Earth being*, an offspring of Earth, not distinct from it. 'Human' tends to imply nowadays a certain separateness and superiority over and above other expressions of life on this planet.

The vital energy of the power animal is there as your vehicle of incarnation. Every person on the path of incarnation enters into the elemental spirit of Earth. In this sense, the power animal represents the energy you require to incarnate on Earth — the force which pulls and keeps you here, as if magnetically attached to Earth. And today, it does not matter how an individual experiences this elemental, incarnational energy. It does not matter whether it configures itself for you as a particular animal, or not. For it is always there, and there is always an aspect of this universal energy which belongs to each spirit, to each person, as they draw closer to life on Earth. It is a very mobile, vital energy; as such, it can at times seem to move away and desert you, leaving you prone to illness. This is why, traditionally, shamans have always attended to their power animal and been aware of its presence. Since the power animal represents Earth's spirit, shamans have always recognized the need for their relationship with it to be constant and intense.

Your power animal represents your own intimate contact with Earth's elemental spirit. This vital spirit possesses a knowledge, a way of knowing, which could bring a much greater sense of attunement to your own personal life on Earth, if it could just be joined with, ridden, and experienced. Like many animals, who know when it is time is to go off and die, without regret, so too with the human being. With this natural, instinctive awareness, you would have an understanding of life and death, which would carry much less fear and remorse—much more of a sense of knowing intuitively what's what, what 'the time' is for.

It is this more conscious relationship with life—and death—on Earth which is going to be so essential in the coming age. For with the blinkered mainstream view that life on Earth is the only form of life in the universe, humankind has been unable to appreciate just how special life on Earth is, in relation to the rest of the universe. With greater awareness of other forms of life in the universe, people will also have a far greater sense of privilege, excitement, and wonder, at this particular, magnificent way of experiencing the universe through life on Earth. They will sense much more of an inner need, or intimate desire, to nurture their relationship with Earth' spirit in whatever way it presents itself to them. Call it your vitality, call it your power animal, it is whatever or however you experience that natural force which binds you to life on Earth, and which makes you want to enter more deeply into it. Of course, this energy may be able to move away from the planet, and journey into other realms. But its focus, its purpose, is to nourish the life of the individual whilst on Earth. Even if the journeys that you make with your power animal take you to the other side of the universe, they are always carried out with the purpose of bringing back to Earth the riches needed to help and to heal, to bring down to the ground the gift of healing.

So whether or not you feel you have a power animal, in the more traditional, shamanic sense, it does not matter. For it is a fact of life that everyone possesses the vital energy of Earth's spirit; and if you do not experience it, it can be brought closer to you through this simple change in your thinking — in your understanding of the specialness and uniqueness of life on Earth.

The dignity of embodiment

The spirit of shamanism brings back an awareness of the awesome power of Earth in which you partake, of which you partake. Would you rather have the comfort and so-called security of a safe position within your social structures, or experience that massive dignity and power of your very own embodiment? One of the gifts of the shaman today can be to bring a much more majestic experience of being alive on Earth back into the mainstream. People can rediscover what it is to be a human animal, in the sense that the elephant or giraffe — or any other creature — carries the majesty and dignity of its species. So the human species can now grow into the dignity and majesty of its own creatureness, its own embodiment. No longer fractured by the isolated, and isolating cells of self, continually wanting to split apart, each individual can know that they are vital to the species as a whole.

Many people within your culture have returned to Earth at this time to begin to taste again the nobility, grandeur, fullness, and in many ways, awesome experience of embodiment, which over aeons has been eclipsed by the artificial structures of your so-called civilizations. Over and over again, the dignity of being human has been flattened by the energies which would have you not incarnate fully and manifest that essential energy of love, which is the point of life on Earth. And love is so much more than sentiment. Rather, it is the experience of shared power, of that shared spirit of Earth coursing through the veins, flowing not only through you, not only through each person, but through every form of manifestation on Earth. It is there to be felt, and to be understood that it belongs to all. It is there to be known that it configures itself for you, as your elemental guardian or power animal, to enable you to express the dignity and grandeur of embodiment upon Earth.

The communal self
The shaman as a spirit is calling very much for a new understanding of who and what you are. It is asking you to realize that consciousness can be focused on the individual, but in essence it cannot be *of* the individual. Consciousness does not belong to the individual. It is a stream — a living, flowing stream — which may be channeled into the form of experience which we call 'the individual.' But it belongs to the sea of awareness with its myriad forms of expression. Understanding this may help you when you feel trapped in mundane life and want to burst open like the flower in the garden. The flower in the garden has its roots in the earth, seeks the sun, drinks the dew, breathes in the light and breathes out the air. It cannot exist except through a celebration of the community of all the spirits which gather in order to manifest that flower. And it is an identical process with each human being. There is absolutely no difference. The human being simply could not exist without the co-operation of all the dimensions and levels of experience — all the forms of life — which converge on that point of celebration which you call 'you.'

There are so many others that make up 'you.' And the stream which gives you consciousness of your self, of 'you,' is itself channeled from the great universal flow, glinting as a reflection, so that you can say 'I,' and 'my.' There could be no other expressi of life like that manifestation of creation which you (could be no other form of experience like your journey this life. It is unique. But it is made possible by so many oth as the life of your culture is made possible, both by you and also by so many others. And your culture itself is a living, growing being.

You are not the beginning, nor the ending.

The ritual space of the body

The modern shaman may wish to undertake rituals which have been used in the past, and that is perfectly valid for the individual who needs those rituals. But there is also a new level of awareness, whereby all the forces which come together in the body are experienced as engaging in a communal ritual, celebrating life. All the elements come together in the body to create a physical point, or focus, of coherence. It is here that the new shaman can enact his or her new ritual within the body—through the awareness and engagement with its rhythmic song of celebration. It is truly physical. The miracle of physical incarnation is the new shaman's terrain, the elevation of awareness of all the participating life forms, which as a community make up the physical body. In this sense, the body is like a tribe, but in a deeper, broader, more elemental sense. For a person's physical body is not simply human. While it *is* a human body, it is also made up of beings that do not belong to the human stream of evolution. For example, much of the body is made up of water, and the elementals that create, sustain and maintain those liquids are not human.

It is through the physical body that each person can be truly embedded in planet Earth. It is a form of 'elemental ecstasy,' but not in the traditional shamanic sense of flying out of the body. It is 'ecstasy' in the sense of moving more deeply, lightly and coherently *into* it, into the communal life of that focus of incarnation, which the physical body is. So your body is no longer a symbol of your separateness from others; rather, it is an experience of utter participation with the life of planet Earth. As such, a ritual space needs to be made in daily life—an imaginative space—to experience the deep, deep, gentle, slow rhythm of this planet, of which the physical body is a part. It is needed in order for Earth's spirit to experience itself more consciously as your body. It is so important to realize and repeat this: the physical body is as much part of the living Earth, as a plot of land, a stone, a tree, a flower, or a bird. This has been forgotten, so that human consciousness has hovered around the body. Now it needs to make that journey into it and to stay there for as long as the experience of life in physical incarnation on Earth requires. This is so important at this time—to awaken to this deep, deep, celebratory awareness of the aspect of Earth, which your body is. It has been your blind spot. It is that gaping hole which so many seek to fill in so many, often artificial ways. It is not even a question of landing on Earth, but of planting yourself within it. *That* is what the shaman is about today.

Today the demands of everyday life and the needs of your culture seem to pull you out of this awareness, away from that imaginative space, where you are able to breathe with the Earth. This is where a new culture could begin: with nothing special, with no special cause, except to be more aware, to expand and extend awareness, not only outwards, but also into the community of awareness and experience, which the physical body itself is.

Shifting to Earth's rhythm

Perhaps when the opportunity arises to enter into this deeper sense of life on Earth, if the thought crosses your mind that this or that is *the* way to go about it—in other words, if the old, old tendency crops up to pin down a path as being *the* path, the right path, the only path—remember that this creates a tension which narrows your openness to the wider, deeper rhythm of the planet. This openness works through acceptance, and the deeper that acceptance is, the more wholehearted your ability is to accept that each person comes to the point they need to come to in their own time and in their own way. As you accept this, then you will be able to breathe more in attunement with the unfolding rhythm of the planet as a whole. And this is true healing, this synchronizing of rhythms. This is the true sense in which awareness and contact with planet Earth is a healing contact. For as you experience that participation, that breathing together, it heals the split, the fractured rhythm and tempo, the out-of-sync relationship.

So there is a close relationship between judgement and health, between the narrowing or tightening of your natural rhythm or frequency, and disease; and the place to begin to heal the dis-ease is within that tribal sense of the self, and especially within that blend of the human and non-human, which is the life of the body as tribe.

CHAPTER 11

AN AGENT OF THOUGHT

Every time you look into the sky and see the stars, and you think 'they are so far away,' there is no way that what you perceive, or what you think of, can be far apart. For in that moment of conception, in that moment of thought, things come together. The miracle of thought brings energies closer together. Once this genuine power has been recognized, then the shamanic quest — the shamanic search for power — will be complete, because the energy and power of thought will have moved the shaman's role on from the need to navigate astral worlds to the ability to be an agent of thought.

This is not saying that one role is better than the other. It is just that working with astral energies has been the dominant experience of humankind for millennia; and apart from by the few — by certain mystics and disciplined adepts — the power of thought has not yet been fully understood or grasped. This is the new, great power initiation which humanity as a whole is approaching — the move beyond the manipulation of energies in the astral worlds into the realm of thought. It does not mean an end to all the color and drama of the astral dimension, but simply that it will not be the focus. It will not be the main theme of human life. There will be less of a need to polarize issues in order to lay out the spectrum of colors within a realm of experience, between the beginning and the ending of a story. The colors will all be there. They will simply be enjoyed, rather than being the area in which issues are thrashed out, the terrain through which life is carved out.

The whole unfolding of humanity in relation to life on Earth will be able to take place in greater maturity. It is like saying that adulthood is no better or worse than adolescence, for they are each realms of experience. But one moves from adolescence into adulthood in the same way that one moves from the astral into the domain of thought. And this is the trend of movement, the possible unfolding of humanity as a whole into the future.

So the new shaman will be much less a navigator of astral worlds and more involved in understanding and handling the rhythms and flow of energy throughout the worlds from a more composed perspective of mind. Human beings will be as much the composers of their experience—the co-creators—as simply the actors.

The dislocation of consciousness
The spirit of shamanism, in a very true but broad sense of shamanism, is about the realignment of human consciousness with all other forms of consciousness on the planet. It is a realignment which is being orchestrated and enacted by the overseers of life on this planet—the devas and guardians of life on Earth. It brings that gift of deeper incarnation to the whole of humanity, and that awareness of the whole.

For aeons, the relationship between humankind and spirit has been one in which human consciousness has been squeezed out of its natural alignment with the universe of spirit. During the long, frozen millennia of the last ice age, a misalignment was forced, not only upon human consciousness, but upon the whole of Earth's consciousness as it embarked upon its 'trial by ice.' The natural direction for energy to flow is from the wider, non-physical universe, through into the physical, and then back out again into 'the worlds beyond.' But throughout human history, there has been a short circuit of this flow, which has blocked wholehearted incarnation. The human spirit has been unable to express itself fully—wholeheartedly—at the physical level. The contraction of human consciousness during the ice age resulted in it being 'twisted out of line.' Instead of being centered on the heart, it was forced *out*, towards the periphery of the body, so that it became located in the extremity of the physical brain. With this focusing, forcing, and concentration of consciousness into the brain, has come the distortion of your ability to experience where you are on

Earth, while you are here, in a more holistic, balanced, peaceful, and holy way. Through this dislocation of consciousness, the Western mind has become blind to the very nature of consciousness itself—of how your whole being is informed by it, rather than you possessing it, in your head.

The shaman's path of pain

In the early days of shamanism, it was as if the shaman had retained an atavistic gift or faculty, which had gradually been lost to others as their consciousness contracted. It was an open awareness of the living presence within every manifestation of life on Earth, within the earth and the skies. But for the ice-age shaman this all changed. For they too eventually succumbed to this misalignment of the mind. Instead of seeing spirit within the physical world itself, the shaman was forced to find it in the non-physical, astral realms. It became necessary for them to fly out of the body in order to work and communicate directly with the world of spirit. For spirit now seemed to have withdrawn beyond the physical, beyond the touch of the fingertips, or sensing it in the leaf on a tree. The shaman had to fly into the astral worlds to seek spirit. Within the astral worlds, as before in the physical world, the connectedness of everything could be seen. The inherent pulse of Earth's consciousness could be felt, now amplified as power, the power of the shamanic quest.

Pain and suffering became the route for the ice-age shaman's deeper engagement with the universe of spiritual energies. For the misalignment of consciousness meant that the shaman had to move forcefully and often painfully against the natural direction of flow of energy into physical life. They had to wrench consciousness away from the physical body in order to blast through that sense of being cut off from spirit. Using drugs or the drum, they propelled their consciousness through this barrier or threshold in order to achieve that greater freedom of awareness and sense of participation with life on Earth. But it could only be achieved out of the body—this temporary realignment of consciousness with Earth's spirit.

A realignment of the mind

Today there is a real transition and a gentle revolution taking place in humanity's spiritual awareness—a relocation of spirit and the realignment of the mind *physically* with the body. The great revolution taking place today is the understanding that spirit not only permeates every atom of life in the universe, but may be seen and perceived as such. It takes very little—apart from an inner sidestep, or mental shift—to move to a position where this can be understood. And as it is understood, then once again spirit can fill up people's lives, where before it had been blocked.

While it is important to be aware of this realignment, of the reconnection of the physical with the spiritual, it is not as important as the *very fact* that this shift is taking place—at a physical, cellular level—this realignment of the total human being right down to the very minute elements which make up a human being. Since it is happening *regardless* of whether one person or another can perceive it, all it requires is the waking up to the fact that it is happening, and indeed, that it has happened. Reality can be perceived more completely and wholeheartedly, without any great spiritual endeavors, or paths of pain and suffering, as has often been the case in the past.

Throughout human history, the majority of people have had to depend in a child-like way upon the spiritual mediators—the priests and the shamans—to maintain their contact with the worlds of spirit. The great shift today is, in a sense, towards the democratization of spirituality. As each person awakens within their mind to an understanding of their relationship with the physical Earth, and to the wider universe of spirit, then through that understanding they will have less and less need for the special individual who in the past has had privileged access to the worlds of spirit.

From the astral to the physical

In the astral worlds, manifest power is the main expression of that level of awareness—the glamor and the drama; and today it is still appropriate for some, even many people to experience that kind of empowerment as part of their own path of learning. But it is almost impossible to describe how much has changed since the need for the shaman evolved. The human community has discovered the power within the physical atom. They know its destructiveness. Now they need to experience it as a living, creative force within each cell and each atom of their physical body. So much has changed. All it needs is the awareness that this power is there. It no longer needs the great quest, or self-denial—the suffering, deprivation and rupturing of normality—as it did in the past, when shamans sought the power of the astral atom and of the astral power animal. There is power within the tiniest cell in the body. And when the spirit withdraws from the body, that power also goes with it, and the body is taken back into the body or atmosphere of Earth, to be re-charged and re-manifest. It is this cellular imagination which needs to awaken—the organic imagination. And the first step is to know that it exists; for that is how most other forms of life on Earth exist—primarily within their organic imagination. The flower is never distinct from the root or the stem, and the human imagination only truly bears fruit within the full awareness and acknowledgement of the root and stem.

The world of organic imagination, and not simply the astral worlds, was the world of the first shamans. For those shamans, the sap and the spirit of life *were* the same thing. Their mind and heart coalesced with the waney edge, the growing point within the tribe, to animate their social body with growth. And today anyone, no matter what they call themselves, who enters into the life of the wider, large tribe of humankind as an animating force of growth, with its life-generating heat, is also a shaman.

Healing into the future

Let your mind just gently dissolve the preconceptions which you bring from your everyday perception and sense of need.

Indeed there is much which can be communicated from this level towards healing as a general reorientation of the mind in human culture. It will take you into a new terrain, with a sense of newness and a message which can uplift and reveal. For this communication, we need to approach the full panoramic vision of past, present and future, in terms of the shaman and shamanism.

In the future, the shaman will not necessarily need to be that specialist of the past, who has always ventured into the astral dimension by leaving the physical body. This is a technique which is valid for those who still need to explore that dimension and understand it more deeply. The skilful 'astral' shaman will discover and reveal those areas in which an individual has suffered soul-loss, where they have been deprived and wrenched away from an integrated position, from the experience of their deeper and more whole self. They will find the causes of pains. They will uncover spirits of sicknesses, and they will seek to join those dislocated aspects of the human being back to their physical focus and location in the everyday world.

Now this book is proposing a new vision of shamanism, and this vision suggests that humanity as a whole is entering into a new era, a new climate of experience. We have described this as an era of thought, where the mind and the realm of thought begin to succeed the long millennia in which the astral dimension and the emotions have been the prime medium of experience. With the movement into this new climate of experience, it will gradually become apparent that more and more people, who had not conceived of themselves as shamans, or even healers, have the capacity to use their minds for the purpose of healing others, and themselves. The ability to do this will come through this realignment of mind and thought with the physical body, which has for so long been out-of-sync and un-integrated.

The emphasis during the course of human history has been upon thrashing around in the astral worlds, seeking solutions in areas where solutions — which require a shift to a new level of awareness — do not exist. In that sea of emotion, there can only be the experience of that emotion. In order to find understanding, there needs to be a movement onto a finer frequency of awareness, which we are calling the realm of thought.

This realm is not new; it has always been there, for, of course, it is part of the make-up of the universe. It is a level of consciousness which is an aspect of all creation. But as the human being now realigns towards the physical, the brain is going to become more active as a vehicle of thought. *And not only the brain.* For it is going to be more and more part of human experience to realize that every aspect of the physical body is capable of thought, not simply the brain. The whole physical body thinks, is conscious at its own level. As the mind realigns with the physicality of life, human beings will not be so trapped in their heads. For this is where, so far, conscious thought has managed to manifest for the vast majority of the human population. The rest of the body has remained under the less conscious influences of astral energies, and been dominated by them.

As an agent of thought, the human being, the new 'shaman' — for this is what we are talking about, the new shaman as a representative of the human race — will be capable of more holistic thought. Thinking will be more like an ambience, an experience within the ambience of their whole physical being, rather than a function or activity confined to the head and the brain. This is the main, radical change for the future — to experience thought both as an ambience, an auric experience, and also right through into the physicality of the human body. Thought is around you and within you, in the cells of your body, in your nerves and blood vessels, in your breathing, in your heartbeat, and not simply in your head.

Now this new conception of thought in relation to the human body also has radical consequences for the future healing of disease. For it is not an over-exaggeration to suggest that much disease of the modern era represents the final letting go, the final cry or 'fling' of this more astral mode of experience, where the shadow energies have held the heart of humankind in such a grip for so long, creating extremes of experience. So the epidemic of degenerative diseases which now sweeps through the whole of your Western culture may be seen to represent the final whip-lash, death-cry, or *rigor mortis* of an era, dominated by fear running through that astral dimension.

After the second World War, when a large part of humanity had been ravaged by one of the deepest and most devastating manifestations of the shadow energies, by what many people have called 'evil,' there was a new sense of hope for the future, the glimmering and dawning that a new beginning could be made. But the hope was that a new era could begin without actually having to change within. All the ills were seen as outside the individual, as the enemy. It needed the last half of the 20th century to finally come to realize that transformation has to take place within, rather than simply building a new world physically—a new material world on the same basis as before. That 'New Age' awareness became a movement which has surfaced in mainstream culture— the awareness that spirit and soul are the foundation of life, not something tacked onto it incidentally, as an after-thought of the scientific mind. As with any powerfully positive surge, there has been a negative backlash to this impulse, bringing further devastation of the global environment. This backlash has been paralleled in human health by the epidemics of degenerative disease, heart disease, cancer, arthritic and immune disease, since the end of the last World War.

One way to understand these diseases is to acknowledge that within them lay the seeds for the future. For they represent, within the physical body, the final degeneration of an era characterized by pervasive emotionality, by the dominance of astral energies, and, more significantly, by the shadow energies of fear. The prevalence of fear is the residue surfacing for the last time before humanity enters the new, more stable, mental realm of experience. So in many ways, degenerative diseases reflect a culture which has been degenerating, not in a moral sense, but in a more organic sense. The primary mode of experience, certainly within Western culture, is dropping away, and this more mental approach is emerging. This is a powerfully collective process, so that throughout this planet, the negative, emotional or 'astral' energies will no longer necessarily be dominant. But as this realignment takes place, there is also a counteraction with the shadow forces trying to grip and hold on. They take hold as degenerative disease. In this respect, there should be absolutely no kind of moral judgement of those who are affected by these diseases (nor should there be of *any* disease). These are apocalyptic times in the sense that the changes taking place now are more fundamental than at any time before in human history.

Proper nourishment
Many see the cure for much modern degenerative disease in terms of diet, and this is very true and accurate in the sense of laying the right soil within the human frame for a new awareness. There is a great cry for fresh food, for proper nourishment, and this is why diet at the physical level is so important. But the cry for fresh food and nourishment does not only concern health and healing at the purely physical level. For it is also a symbolic cry for proper food and nourishment for the soul and the spirit. People want, more and more, organic sustenance. And this is what the spirit of shamanism is about. For the new shamanic healing is to do with the nourishment which Earth's spirit brings, when more fully aligned to human consciousness.

Proper nourishment and fresh food in the coming era means not only the right kind of vegetable, or grain, or meat. It also means that accord between the human soul and Earth's aura—that expansion of awareness which allows the human soul and spirit to move more freely within the deeper, slower ambience of Earth's spirit. Proper food and nourishment is when the human soul and spirit breathe out from the confines of brain consciousness into the whole body consciousness, and then out into the whole Earth consciousness.

As the mind realigns to be more in tune with the physical body, and as that cellular imagination awakens and extends beyond the human frame out into Earth's being, then thought, in its moment of conception, will instantly be able to heal. It will need no great rituals, no great endeavors, no heroic, monumental undertakings, but simply that breathing out of the fragment of self into Earth's wider being. For Earth is a planet of healing. It is a planet of nourishment. In essence, it is a planet of abundance, and that abundance, first and foremost, is to do with the healing of poverty of spirit. So in that moment of thought there is the potential for cells to change and for disease to be contained. This kind of thought is not simply from the head. It is thought which comes from the whole being of that person who wishes for healing. In a sense, this is a new, 'shamanic' form of prayer, where the new shamanism entails the journey into the physical cell, the elemental physicality of the body. In this new vision of shamanism, this is possibly the most radical change—the shaman's journey, not into other worlds beyond the physical, but into the very worlds which make up the physical, which exist here and now within this domain of experience, and which call for this new alignment to be attended to.

So this new form of shamanic healing, will be available—is available—in the twinkling of an eye. And as the collective mind of your culture changes, so there will be greater receptivity towards this form of healing, which may begin to manifest spontaneously. The most fertile soil for this new form of healing will be the awareness that it can happen; and although it can happen without that fertile awareness, it will become the norm when this shift in the collective human psyche is complete.

CHAPTER 12

SPIRIT AND 'THE SPIRITS'

Each person has an essence which makes them uniquely themselves, and it is this essential self which is often referred to as 'the spirit.' Now language is always changing through time, whereas communication at other levels beyond time does not necessarily need language or the use of concepts in such a highly defined way as you do. The use of the word 'spirit' can make your essential self sound like some small spark of light, which you possess, and this may be one way of visualizing it. But at the same time it is also a great field of experience, it is your larger self, of which 'you' are a part. Your larger self exists mainly out of time, but an aspect of it dips in to the experience of time and physicality. In a certain sense, when you dip in, you become a 'person,' whereas in your larger self, you belong to a populace, a sphere of experience and existence which is 'peopled,' although not in the same way as on Earth.

So it may be helpful to look upon your spirit, your essence, in this larger, spatial sense, as your more expanded self, existing on a finer frequency of life than the physical. The more refined your essence becomes, the more all pervasive and all embracing it becomes, until, ultimately, at its most refined level, it is everywhere and in everything. You merge back into the source of life itself, often called 'God' or 'the Godhead,' which goes everywhere, and into everything.

The world 'beyond'
So one way of looking at your spirit is as a field — a field of intelligent energy with its own coherence. Another way is to conceive of it as a spark, and this is much more the way in which it has come to be viewed as a result of life on Earth. For through incarnation, there is this sense of the narrowing and concentration of one's

being. If you take the view that planet Earth, and every form of life on it, including the human race, has been going through an experience of being ruled by fear, then this ambience of fear has contracted the spirit, or, rather, it has contracted the way in which you experience spirit into this sense of it being a spark, almost like a fragment itself. This is why when a person dies and leaves their physical body, people say 'their spirit has left them.' The spirit has left the body, and 'gone back' to wherever it is thought to have come from. There has been this notion of heaven as being a far away place, far from life on Earth. But if you take the more expanded view of the spirit—as being a vibration, or a unique *field* of intelligent energy—then death may be seen simply as a process of widening again the band of your experience back onto its natural frequency; your focus, or consciousness, shifts back into its more naturally expanded field, whereas it has had to adapt and contract in order to enter into life on Earth.

So in many ways, death is the relocation of consciousness back into that expanded field of awareness, or frequency of consciousness, where to a large extent you already are. The only difference now is the alteration in that field as a result of the experience you gained in incarnation. What has often been called 'the world beyond,' is a frequency of life and awareness, which has always encompassed and, in a sense, 'infiltrated' your life on Earth, except that now, during incarnation, it has become the background setting for that life, rather than the focus of it. With death there is simply a re-focusing of consciousness, and an expansion into one's wider, deeper, broader self, or spirit.

In order to experience life on Earth, there has to be a kind of concentrated 'squeezing' of the self into the physical. But with that contraction of spirit comes a loss of consciousness or awareness, the loss of memory of one's non-physical, expanded self. With this reawakening to Earth's spirit, the human mind will come to understand more deeply its own essential nature, so that its immersion in physicality will also be understood as an immersion in a form of spirit.

Death and the power animal
Many people suffer a lot when they die, and the fear of this suffering is one of the greatest fears limiting human life on Earth. It has dominated human life throughout recorded history. To be fair, part of this fear is natural—that fear which comes from the trauma when the forces creating and maintaining your current form are loosened and dissolved. This can be a shock for the incarnating aspect of your spirit, and a source of fear for you in your physical consciousness. But this is where contact with the power animal, and an awareness of its role in incarnation can help. As the force which binds you to life on Earth, the power animal is also the force which releases you. It is very much in direct communication with those elementals who maintain your physical form and physiological processes. So the power animal, as your link with Earth's spirit, enables you to be involved, not only in your own incarnation, but also in your own process of leaving physical life. It binds you and releases you—it is a natural process.

Just as most people in Western culture are generally unaware of their power animal, of the energy which binds them to Earth's spirit, so they are also unaware of it as the energy which helps them to loosen that bond enabling them to move away from life on Earth. Shamans have tended to understand these processes. They have usually gone through a kind of death experience themselves—even if not physical death—and gained access to the levels at which these formative forces operate. This was the special skill of the shaman as psychopomp, to lead a person's soul and spirit away from life in the physical body, back towards an awareness of the population which exists out of incarnation. Today, with greater understanding of the energies binding you to life on Earth—which we are calling the 'power animal'—it will be possible for people, not only to live life more deeply and fully, but also to die more fearlessly, for their consciousness will have become more organic, and they will have become more fully aware of the processes of life and death.

What you call the 'natural' fear of dying often has more to do with the fear of losing control over your life. It also has to do, to some extent, with that elemental fear of dissolving the forces which hold you in shape and enable you to be here as you are in your current form. But this growing awareness of Earth's spirit will enable incarnation to be gentler, and so the process of dying may also be gentler.

With their artificial sense of time, many people have lost touch with the natural rhythms and cycles of growth and decay on Earth. They have forgotten that there is a 'natural' time for all these things—Earth's time. Once these rhythms and cycles are felt and understood again, there will be a loosening of this fear of death. With the regained awareness that soul and spirit are the basis or foundation to all experience in the universe, and with a greater awareness of the spirit's purpose in incarnation, there will be less regret at the length of a person's life, whether it's long or short. There will be the understanding that a person is here for as long as they *need* to be, and that this is something which Earth's spirit—configuring itself as the power animal—*knows* in each case. The same forces which bind you here are usually very instrumental in the manner and process through which you are released, even if they sometimes look unnatural, as in an accident.

As the mind becomes more aligned to the purpose of life in the physical body, to its own physicality and its elemental sharing with every other form of life on Earth, there will a deeper understanding that consciousness can exist in many domains, and is not tied to the physical form. It is universal, cosmic, galactic. Consciousness permeates the universe in its myriad fields of awareness. These fields of awareness are what you understand as 'spirit,' or 'spirits.' The freedom which many people yearn for is the freedom which they already know and have in their deeper, spiritual selves. It is something which they will be able to experience more consciously—even whilst still on Earth in the body—when this realignment of thought and physicality has fully taken place. Death will be understood merely as a shift in one's perception, in many ways into a more familiar, unencumbered kind of life, where there is much more of a remembering 'what it's all about.'

As the fear of death itself recedes, so the tension which helps to create many diseases will not be so intense. It will also make the process of dying gentler and able to take place with greater understanding. The language which you use for dying may have helped people in the past to come to terms with it, but it has not truly helped to move your understanding forwards. Concepts such as 'moving on,' 'departing,' 'going away,' do not really grasp the fact that it is just a simple shift, and that it is not as if you have gone *anywhere* far away at all.

As your mind realigns, you will realize that time only exists in a certain sphere of experience, and that space is the medium in which you paint the colors of your lives in time. But the concepts of 'far' and 'near' will gradually become redundant, since the contents of each thought exist within the same moment, and along the same coordinates of that thought, allowing them to overlap and coexist. The seeming 'laws' of the physical world will be seen as the exception rather than the rule.

The shaman's spirits

The concept of 'spirit' has never been truly abandoned by human societies, despite all the efforts to rationalize it away in the modern era. The spirituality of tribal societies has always been based upon it, and upon their understanding and acceptance of 'the spirits.' Each tribe generally has its own local pantheon of invisible forces or beings, which permeate their universe, and with whom the shaman negotiates on their behalf. Today, with the revival of shamanism in Western society, there is often confusion as to whether your culture also possesses such 'spirits.'

For the traditional shaman, the first and most obvious group of 'the spirits' are just people, but who are no longer physically alive. Most tribal shamans have drawn on the perspective of these spirits for wisdom and information. These are either people they have known, or ancestors who have been in close association with the tribe at some point in its history. In this sense, these spirits are just people; and they may not necessarily be that much wiser, or have that much of a better perspective on things than those in incarnation. The greater power which comes from being 'dead' — 'power' in the sense of freedom from limitation — have made many tribal peoples hold the so-called 'dead' in awe. Of course, many of these people may well be very wise, and serve as guides and inspiration for those in physical life. Like your own personal guide, they may be concerned with your life, and move to influence your life in a way which, in a sense, you have agreed with them already, prior to your incarnation. But the idea that you can hand your life over to *the* spirits' and let them get on with it — it's almost like saying you are prepared to hand your life over to your family or friends, and let *them* get on with it! It's not the same as saying you will hand your life over to the Tao, to the Godhead, or to the flow of universal intelligence. For, in a way, those same helping spirits are subject to the same guiding principles as everyone else — to the Tao, for example — even though they are out of incarnation. Some of these spirits can see further than you can see, and may be helpful; but in no way are they infallible. Looking for certainty is only something you can find within yourself — the certainty of your own essence. The spirits are there to guide and advise, maybe, but they are not there to live your life for you or pre-empt your own decisions. They can point you in a certain direction. But they cannot act for you, unless you give yourself over to them and ask them to act for you, which is more like possession than co-creation.

Nor are they are to be worshipped or held in awe. For everyone in incarnation also possesses that potential for greater wisdom. Being available to the tribe means that these discarnate guides have to remain, to some extent, within the astral realms, either the higher astral realms in the case of the wise guides, or the lower astral realms when it is a case of more fear-bound or mischievous influences. Sometimes they are there to help, sometimes maybe not. Basically they are just like you or anyone else, except that they are no longer in a physical body. So they are one aspect of 'the spirits.'

Animal and elemental spirits
Then there are those animal spirits and power animals, who are another group of 'the spirits.' Again, it is easy to elevate these energies. As we have already seen, the power animal is an essential influence on human life in the process of incarnation, as well as in dying. There is a much deeper, closer, more intimate link between human beings and other animals than your present culture recognizes, which is expressed in the legends of half-human, half-animal beings. Out of incarnation, there is less of a separation between these kingdoms, since those 'people' — those beings or spirits, who take the form of animals in their physical lives — are hardly different at all from you at that deep level of spirit. That is why shamanic peoples often talk of 'tree people,' or 'animal people,' because they realize that, inhabiting that *expression* of life is a spiritual being, essentially like yourself.

Another level of 'the spirits' is that of the more purely elemental energies, such as the spirits of water. Some are more deva-like in the sense that they might oversee a wider range of expressions of life. They are a more all-embracing manifestation, similar, or closer, if you like, to the angels, and to the gods and goddesses.

All that is happening is that, as you evolve, you have the capacity to permeate or interpenetrate far more comprehensive levels and expressions of life. At the ultimate level, you are everywhere, in everything. But having taken on this particular form of physical life, you have a life that exists in time, with a beginning and an end. To the extent that those who are out of incarnation ally themselves to those living in physical life, they are partly affected by your sense of passing time. They can dip down closer. But there is much less of a difference between you and most of 'the spirits' than you generally think. They need to be distinguished. They need a new, more mature level of being met, rather than trusted simply because they are invisible. Not everything which is invisible can be trusted any more than everything that is visible can be trusted. With your consciousness immersed in physicality and in passing time, you often lose awareness of the spiritual universe beyond the physical. But it is a universe more accurately described simply as 'non-physical,' since the physical world is also 'spirit.'

New living presences

Most traditional, tribal cultures have their own pantheon of spirits, which are recognized or understood as real, even if they are only perceived by the shaman during their journey or shamanic flight, and not by other members of the tribe. In this sense, '*the* spirits' is a concept which is appropriate for these cultures, which have their own shared understanding of them. They are invisible forces permeating the lives of tribal peoples—forces which they are accustomed to, and have given names to. These spirits are often very rooted in the lands which the tribal peoples have inhabited over long periods of time. The names of the spirits are commonly tied to particular places. This is why the loss of their ancestral lands threatens not only the physical but also the spiritual survival of tribal peoples—it threatens their whole being.

In the Western revival of shamanism, these ancestral spirits of place tend to be overlooked. They have been forgotten, and this is one important reason why you need to question the language you use today. When the modern, Western shaman talks of '*the* spirits,' where do they reside? Even if the physical locations in which they used to be found have been forgotten, do they still reside in the collective mind? Are these spirits part of a shared understanding? Do they belong to your culture as a whole, as a pantheon of invisible forces, or are they purely personal guides? If they are purely personal spirit guides, then it is surely grandiose to speak of them as '*the* spirits.'

Because your own culture lacks the traditional, shamanic understanding of energies beyond the physical, it has no names or history for them. As a result, it is in a tremendous state of potential. It is the potential not so much for creating a new local pantheon of spirits, as of using concepts which are far more expansive and all embracing to refer to the invisible forces which intimately affect your lives. The concepts of science, for example, have gone some way to refer to invisible forces, except that most scientists still refuse to give these forces that animating quality, which is a fundamental characteristic of 'spirit.' Scientific concepts like gravity, relativity, and so on, have tremendous potential, once their animating and ensouling qualities are perceived and understood as being also within them. They are not just abstract concepts referring to forces, they are living energies—*living presences* is perhaps the closest and most suitable way of describing such 'spirits.' You need an understanding of spirit that takes you into the future, that rides the rising tidal waves of scientific thought which have given birth to modern culture. An awareness of spirit can expand that thinking and infuse the scientific universe with life.

It would be helpful to see the shamanic concept of '*the* spirits' as belonging to tribal cultures, who have their own very distinct cultural spirituality and pantheon of spirits—and their own places where the spirits live. The difficulty which many Western people have with inheriting this concept, and even with your own concept of spirit, is that these words are too vague and insubstantial. Today the word 'energy' is often used to describe the many levels, and the many vibrations or frequencies of life, both in and out of incarnation. For some people it is a more comfortable term than 'spirit,' since it is more attuned to the scientific concepts of your own culture.

There is much to come in your understanding. Your world is on the verge of a new understanding and language for talking about these things; and the gentle revolution in your relationship between physical and non-physical existence will bring forth a new language.

CHAPTER 13

ECHOES OF FUTURE GRACE

This communication is very much for healing — to understand how seeking wholeness does not necessarily mean healing every single ailment or problem. An illness, like cancer, for example, may be understood as part of the process of becoming whole. It will express itself individually as the disease which that person needs in order to balance out the wider, deeper process of their spiritual evolution over many lives. So there is an important distinction to make with any illness between the desire for relief from suffering and the need to go through the process of what that illness is about.

This is why some diseases seem so inexplicable. Why should a small child be afflicted by a terrible, agonizing disease? Neither individual lives, nor individuals' diseases can be truly, deeply understood within the context of a single life, at least not the major life-threatening diseases, nor those which are clearly bringing a person's life to an end. The same applies when people die from heart attacks or accidents. It needs the perspective from up the hill, the overview, to see the pattern of 'the many lives.' The limitation of the concept of a single life brings with it a limited understanding of disease, of the apparent cruelty and mindlessness of certain diseases. When they cannot be viewed from within the spiritual context of the whole, of the bigger, wider story, diseases like cancer remain a mystery, except to the extent that a healer moves beyond the need to understand with the mind to the understanding of the heart. The understanding of the heart brings acceptance and unconditional love to the person suffering illness, and there is no need for answers or explanations. But for those who seek some semblance of an answer, to understand what a major illness like cancer is about, it must lie in that great panoramic view of the whole — the themes which are being lived out over many lives, the stories and the dramas which are being enacted, and the lessons which one person brings to another.

The planet of healing and sound

Earth is very much a planet of healing. When you look around you and see so much disease, this is one of the reasons for it. Many spirits bring their 'dis-ease' to Earth to find a degree of healing. There are many other locations within the universe where more harmonious lives may be lived. But the disharmony on Earth is partly to with its purpose—to heal the disharmony that there may be within one's spirit as it travels its path of evolution. It needs that particular form of healing which may be obtained through dipping down into physical life on Earth. It is a fairly concentrated form of experience, and much of Earth's healing quality has to do with sound.

In a very real sense, Earth is a planet of music and sound. It is a very sound-sensitive planet. Many of the sounds of the natural world have enormously powerful healing qualities—the wind itself, the wind in relation to the trees and other plants, the wind in relation to water, water in relation to the element of earth—all generate or create sound, audible sound, with healing properties; and the inaudible sounds which exist all around the planet act to maintain a healing integrity within the planet itself.

In order to understand the relationship between sound and disease, let us first look at a relatively minor human complaint, that which you call 'tinnitus.' Tinnitus is not really an illness, but it does involve dis-ease relating to sound—a kind of electronic sound which is being perceived as an unwanted intrusion. Part of the problem has to do with the enormous increase in recent years in the level of noise on the etheric level, which is very closely related to all the electronic activity taking place in Earth's atmosphere. As one becomes more sensitive, it can become more difficult to filter out this level of energy. The electronic activity impinges upon the physical-etheric aspect of a person's being, and it is primarily the increase in the level of this activity which causes this interference.

Tinnitus is also partly to do with a build up of psychic energy within the individual, although it is not the psychic energy itself which causes the perception of this sound. Rather it is the pressure which the psychic energy — which is more astral — places upon the etheric, giving it a degree of stress. It is really important in this case to engage in some kind of integrating activity, some form of practice through which all the bodies and the chakras are allowed to merge and integrate more freely and smoothly. Also, at this time, it is important to be able to discharge some of the psychic energy, to release or channel it, perhaps in some form of uninhibited, creative activity — especially involving sound — where you do not judge the results. This kind of 'letting go' can be a health-giving activity, and must not be judged as to whether it is great art, or music, or poetry, or whatever. It can also allow an element of humor to enter into your life, which is vitally healing and is also why it must not be taken too seriously, for it is the ability to discharge the confusion and the pressure, to conduct it away, which is health-giving.

So it is a good idea, from the point of view of health, and of perhaps finding a cure for this problem, to create time and space for some form of discharging activity, which enables this noise to be earthed. For those who smoke and experience tinnitus, nicotine does not help. If you can generate willingness within, without trying to force anything, you may find that smoking can drop away with the necessary degree of willingness. But it must not become a pressure or an anxiety. For fear is one important, underlying cause of certain major diseases like cancer — the fear generated by what you believe other people think or expect of you, or by what 'experts' and 'authorities' tell you to do.

Social pressure and disease
Despite all the widely-advertised physical 'causes' of cancer detected by your scientists, perhaps the most prevalent, and unacknowledged, *cultural* cause is the social pressure — which a person sustains and absorbs — to express themselves as *something which they are not*. This is the pressure to grasp dry, empty straws

which crumble the moment they are grasped. It is the pressure to streamline the many broad, diverse ways of finding fulfillment in life into believing that it must be found through some specific form of outer action. It is feeling impelled to 'do' rather than to 'just be,' to achieve for its own sake, and to find recognition through trying to please certain important others in your life.

Whilst recognition — being known — *is* an important part of the human experience, it does not have to be sought after for its own sake. It will come, the more you allow yourself to be yourself, the more you live your life in its own intrinsic way, at the rhythm and tempo which suits you. Recognition may be found in many, sometimes small, incidental ways, rather than having to be pursued along the one 'important' route. When this is truly understood, there will be an easing up of this disease in your culture. At root, it involves that very profound saying, 'Know thyself,' for if you do not know yourself to be a willow tree you may spend your life trying to be an oak. If you know yourself to be a tall whispering poplar, you will not try to be a majestic pine.

One example of this deep stress which comes from not accepting yourself as you are is the epidemic of breast cancer today amongst women. Symbolically, this has very much to do with the great changes which have already taken place in the role and position of women in society. For a very long time, as part of the overall state of planetary imbalance, the energies of the shadow held women back and down in a position of social isolation and political impotence. To the extent that this position has started to improve now, these same shadow energies have, in a sense, hit back very strongly at women through the body. Despite the greater outer changes in social and political equality between men and women, psychic and psychological imbalance is still common, in both sexes. With this greater outer equality, an even more acute tension has been generated within the female psyche, which fractures the etheric and allows the disease to take hold. For women — more quickly than men — discover the emptiness of achievement in the outer world, when it lacks the fullness of a balanced inner life. This sense of fullness within may come through having children and a family; or it may come through unveiling the riches and treasures within their own psyche. It brings the knowledge of what is truly your own, of the treasure which you, as a woman, possess; and it brings health to your own inner child.

For the many women who seek both to look after a family and also feel driven to achieve something within the world outside the family, a violation often occurs of their own soul child. Your soul child needs to receive unconditional love; it needs to misbehave and not be punished, it needs to run riot. It is the soul child with the mercurial streak, the bubbling out genie, the wild. When it is repressed, it may manifest as physical illness. Many women seeking fulfillment in terms of outer achievement and worldly success often find that they need to adopt the ways and means of a still male-dominated culture to pursue their goals. This can force that soul child into a distortion of its natural shape, and into that prison of achievement, with the pressure of expectation.

Social pressure has far more to do with the creation of disease in your culture than is generally understood—far more so than many supposedly harmful substances. The old saying of 'a healthy mind in a healthy body' assumes that if you look after you body, your mind will look after itself. But this is a reversal of what actually happens. For it is the healthy mind, one which is not torn apart by pressures, injunctions, fears, and the stresses of trends that must be followed, which is much more able to deal with irritants, stimulants, and all the difficult substances which may contribute to, but not cause disease.

The cold fire of cancer

From the broad perspective of the shamanic past, and moving into the future, let us now look in more detail at cancer, and the particular kind of illness that cancer is. For cancer is a kind of illness. It is not a single illness but a type of disease. At one level, cancer is the fire from the spirit, which comes to consume the physical body and release the soul into a new form of life. So for many people it is the way in which death clothes itself; at a very deep level, it has of course been chosen, as well as, to some extent, the degree of suffering. But the terror and pain of having to go through the process of this disease, and the process of release from physical life, is one of the biggest challenges facing any person. There is no right or wrong way to go about it. It is a challenge which calls upon the deepest resources within the individual.

Cancer may be a fire but it is a cold fire—it burns away the link between the spirit and the body, so that the spirit may finally withdraw from the body before, if it chooses, coming back to another one. It is a natural process, in the sense that the processes of nature are adapted in order to close the door on a life, as physical incarnation. There is a break down within the physical body, and the cells start to disrupt and finally end the activity of coherent physical life.

Cancer has existed as a disease process since the beginning of civilization as you understand it, since that time when human beings began to cut their consciousness off from the wider sphere of Earth's being. It became part of the human collective psyche as the forces of nature became introverted into culturally creative drives; and while even small children may have cancer, this is because it touches them and is available to them as a cultural disease. For even a small child is also a spirit, traveling a path of evolution. Through the experience of cancer they may be bringing through certain important qualities which further not only their own spiritual growth but also that of their parents and family.

Cancer and sound
We have seen how important diseases like cancer need the perspective of 'the many lives' to be fully understood. This is their karmic aspect. We have also seen that vulnerability to the social pressures upon an individual to be someone other than who they really are may predispose them towards diseases like cancer. This, in a sense, is their psychospiritual aspect. But what about the external causes, which may trigger the disease, causing it to manifest?

The medical-scientific approach today is to 'fight' the disease as if waging a war. Physical 'causes' are identified, isolated, and the attempt is made to eliminate them. If the 'cause' cannot be isolated and attacked, it is not considered a cause. One example of this is sound. Even though this is something for the future, it is a factor which is overlooked and simply not understood at present. But today's epidemic of cancers, in many ways, has its physical foundation in your world's culture of sound. The massively discordant world in which you live — the sounds which you take in through your deeply intimate sense of hearing, day in and day out — has been playing a very large part in creating what one might call the holes or cracks in the etheric body. This allows the process of disruption of the physical cells to start at the various sites on the body. It is a kind of noise pollution, but not simply in the sense of loud noises. Rather, it is the overall discordant ambience of modern living which is an almost totally overlooked underlying cause of today's cancer epidemic. It is worth those who value their well being to give time to seeking out quiet places on a regular basis, just to be in them, without it hardly mattering what one does in them. What matters is just to be in those spaces, and better still — for those who are able — to inhabit them on a full-time basis.

The pattern is there within the whole of the collective body of humankind; and as the fractures become greater, so the epidemic grows. If your car engine were silent, electric, that would go a very long way to reducing the disruption. While the fumes from your vehicles are harmful, they are not so fundamentally disruptive as the vibration created by the engines, which contributed so much to the 20th and early 21st centuries' epidemic of cancer, more so than many of the other causative factors which have been detected. The engine sounds of this era will seem in future years to have been a massive aberration.

The healing sound
Looking at cancer from this new perspective, how can we move our understanding of it on in a practical way? In the present culture, much is laid on the courage with which people battle against their disease; and sadly, much of this courage is the courage they need, on the one hand, to face the possibility of their

own immanent death, and, on the other hand, the suffering which the illness—and often the treatment—brings. So from this perspective, there is a perceived need for ways to change the minds of those who approach healing and treatment.

The way forward for the treatment of cancers would be, on the one hand, to continue to use surgery where there is an urgent, acute need to act in order to preserve life. But treating the chronic condition requires some form of communication with those cells in the body which have run riot. Communicating with those cells needs, not so much the destructive approach of 'chemical warfare,' as a sonic approach. For science is on the verge of learning how cells respond to sound, and especially to the sound of the human voice. But as the disease process—and also the healing of it—is a profoundly personal and individual process, it is not just a matter of any human voice.

For each person suffering from cancer, there is likely to be, amongst those that they know, one person whose voice has the greatest capacity to heal, so that when a diagnosis of cancer is made, the community will be mobilized. All those within that person's life—past, present and perhaps future—will be called upon, silently, spiritually, and also actually, so that there is a sense of the community drawing closer to that person. Out of that community may come the voice, the sound which that individual person needs in order to restore a sense of balance and harmony to their soul, and therefore to their body. In this way, the fear surrounding the technical treatment of cancer, like surgery, will be reduced, and the isolation currently experienced during the treatment of cancer will be reversed. The concept of healing will extend beyond all the specialists to the very soul of the individual needing healing, and also the soul of the person giving healing, as expressed through the sound of their voice. There will be greater understanding of the need for a certain sound, and of how the sounds of certain voices can both cause and heal disease. This is not a question of good or bad, or right or wrong, for one kind of sound which may heal one person could equally cause illness in another person over a long period. This is a radical, although not new idea. The voice is going to become more and more powerful again, as part of the raising of the energy of this planet. It is already happening. For the time being it needs to happen, in a sense, half-consciously, for if people become over-self-conscious about the sound of their voice, it could block out this healing potential.

So we are looking at cancer as something uniquely individual, and the healing of it also as something very uniquely individual. While it may take considerable time for this understanding of sound to filter through into your mainstream culture, it is the regaining of an ancient, 'lost' art, but one which has always been understood by shamans from the earliest of days.

Sound cannot be applied as a general technique to all cases, nor any sound—especially not electronic sound. For electronic sound can adversely affect the degree to which the etheric body meshes with the physical. Just by being electronic, many sounds can loosen that connection and allow the physical cells in the body to run riot. For cancer is essentially the distortion of the etheric body manifesting physically. This is why words and sounds of power have always been so fundamental to shamanic healing. But it has been misunderstood to some extent with the revival of shamanism into believing that *any* kind of 'shamanic' sound can heal.

Today a person who is suffering from this disease needs to be willing to seek out the sounds which make them feel distinctively better, which give them a sense of harmony. A person being read stories by another individual, whose voice they experience as harmonious and healing, will go a long way towards restoring balance.

So these are some comments on the disease of cancer. To the extent that human beings have made an unnatural response to their position within the natural world, so the cells within their bodies have a tendency to behave unnaturally. For example, Western culture's deeply ingrained belief in unlimited economic growth and development is unnatural and helps to maintain cancer as a disease available within the collective human psyche. Energy follows thought, and not only Earth, but also your bodies, are being devastated by this posture of plunder.

CHAPTER 14

THE VALE OF SOUL-MAKING

Imagine you are on a hill, looking out over a plain, which is populated with towns and cities everywhere. This view represents life on Earth, in the sense of being a valley, the vale of soul-making. Soul-making is usually understood as suffering and pain; and the suffering of mental illness is so much part of that deeply intimate process of allowing the spirit to grow more fully and more deeply in its consciousness and refinement. Soul-making is the expression of that process in incarnation.

Conductors of chaos

In the atmosphere, when a storm is brewing, electric tension builds up. When the storm finally breaks, releasing wind and rain, it does so over the whole community. But that electric charge strikes only in certain places, causing damage and destruction.

Similarly, for many individuals who are mentally ill, they are like those places where lightning has struck. They are taking on and discharging much of the unspoken, unresolved, undischarged, trapped pockets of negative energy, which have built up within the collective human psyche, sometimes over aeons.

In this respect, these people are performing a service for the community and need to be honored for the kind of task which they have taken on in their lives. For it is not just a matter of chance, or 'bad luck.' Often they have become—at a very deep level—the willing conductors of this undischarged astral tension.

Nor is their task always just a matter of living out their personal karma. Theirs may be a form of service to the community, in the same way that the shaman has always performed a service to the community, often sacrificing their own personal life in the process. There are many close links between the shaman's experience of turmoil, and some forms of mental illness; and the greatest change will take place for these people through a change in the understanding of the community—that this minority is enabling the majority to live more stable lives.

The mentally ill may also begin to receive a certain kind of recognition for their role in society, once the whole community has developed a much deeper and more organic understanding of consciousness itself. For consciousness is like a sea, or a medium, flowing through all of creation, filling up the forms and the spaces; and the consciousness of a person experiencing mental illness is made up of the very same 'stuff' as your own self-consciousness.

As the spirit of shamanism reawakens and resurfaces within the human community, more and more people will come to realize that life—including their own awareness and experience—is a totally shared phenomenon, having only individual points of difference. With the understanding that the underlying ground of experience is the same for everyone, you will come more and more to acknowledge both the validity of this particular form of soul-making, and also the necessity for these individuals undergoing it as part of the overall, wider, deeper evolution of the human spirit.

The task force

In much modern mental illness, there is the discharging of residues of a whole massive era of emotionality. Quite often this discharging of negative energy really needs a whole family, rather than just the experience of an isolated individual. Each member of the family, in their own way, can either act out this discharging or help to support and contain the process. In these cases, the experience of mental illness cannot be fully understood as the experience of just one individual; for it is very much a group undertaking. As this group experience radiates out into the wider community, it is diffused. This is very much one of the possibilities within life on Earth—Earth as a planet of sound and healing—this ability to discharge and diffuse pockets of trapped energy through the vehicle of the living Earth. It is as if, for part of their lives, the members of the family incarnate almost like a task force, with the purpose to discharge these energies. Each member of the family has their own, equally important role within this group process. When the task is done, they can move on, each in their own way, whether in or out of incarnation; and because it is such a highly charged situation, it quite often needs extra time to enable the releasing to take place. Once completed, they can move on, each within their own sphere of life. In a certain sense, they can disband, having completed their mission as a group.

The suffering of the shaman
The subject of mental illness goes to the very heart of shamanism; and there is a large pearl to manifest here, a whole realm of experience. It is a terrain which has been trodden by this shaman-sensitive through many lives, gathering around him not only the pain and the burden, which he has carried through those lives, but also the possibility to move awareness and understanding forward.

One of the great skills of the shamans of the past has been to approach the threshold of self-consciousness, and blast through the psychic barrier between everyday brain consciousness and the wider sphere of imperceptible energies around and beyond you. The shaman has been able to journey to what lies *behind* physical manifestation, more so, in a sense, than entering *into* the physicality of life itself. For their experience has been primarily astral. The astral dimension is very much one which underlies the physical expression of life on Earth, although it is by no means the only one. But it creates the color, the display, the richness of life on Earth; and the shaman has generally been very effective in dealing with this realm of experience.

Now in order to break through this psychic barrier between brain consciousness and the wider dimension of astral reality, the shaman suffered. They carried out rituals, and underwent disturbance and turmoil; and through entering into this realm of experience, they often became imbued themselves with the powerfully dramatic, colorful qualities, which characterize the astral worlds. Indeed, theirs was an experience which, if it had become accessible to the whole of humanity, could possibly have led to its destruction.

If all human beings had become 'charged,' as the shaman did, by immersion in the astral worlds, and if they had become so totally dedicated to them, then ordinary grounded human life would have become impossible. Anarchy would have reigned, and the ability of communities to be socially and politically coherent would have been blown apart by this excess of the astral within the physical and social domains. It needed the special individual to be able to maintain the link with these dynamically creative worlds, and to discharge pockets of difficult or dangerous energies, known throughout history as 'evil spirits.' So the shaman took on a role which ensured the survival of the tribe, but which, if it had been taken on by all the members of the human race, would have ensured its destruction.

Today in Western culture, in the absence of this tribal, shamanic awareness, many of the mentally ill unconsciously perform this essential task.

Astral intrusions
Seeing visions and hearing voices which are not perceptible to others was often considered one of the hallmarks of the shaman-to-be. It indicated that this person was open to the worlds of the spirits — that they had a natural propensity to enter the astral dimension of life. In a way, you could say that those worlds push in so strongly upon this kind of individual that they don't have the same degree of concentrated resistance which most other 'normal' people have. Indeed, people with a high level of concentrated resistance today often need to allow themselves to open up and move more out into those worlds they've resisted. They need to break through into the astral dimension, to work more purposefully in dream reality, and experience the shamanic journey. This can be a valuable and necessary part of their path, of their own individual growth — acknowledging, experiencing, and exploring this very powerful and colorful dimension which pushes through into the physical world, bringing forth so many rich expressions of life. They need to see and discover what lies behind those physical expressions.

But for many others, for those who are mentally ill, this pushing or pressing in of the astral worlds dislocates their consciousness. The location of their incarnating spirit is shifted away from the everyday experiences which their own soul is going through. The spirit is forced to withdraw from its position within or near the physical; and it leaves behind the 'residue' of that life and experience — the soul, and the personality — which now suffer these unwanted astral incursions, or 'presentations.'

Generally speaking, the hearing of voices and delusions in schizophrenia are 'presentations' from a certain level or realm of experience within the astral. They come from energies which have not been sufficiently refined, in the sense of being able to blend with the individual. It is as if they have their own agenda. They are 'shadow energies,' in that they give the individual no sense of choice, whereas offerings or incursions from the world of spirit which only enter a person's consciousness freely, when invited, are generally from a more refined level, or 'light' side, of that same astral dimension. So in mental illness, the incursions are unwanted and really are intrusions, while with more balanced 'inspiration' or 'channeling,' they are offered rather than forced.

The shamanic sacrifice

Many people who suffer mental illness are bringing with them from former incarnations a 'natural' ability to move beyond the thresholds of ordinary consciousness. Over their many lives, they may have learned to distinguish between the shadow qualities of compulsion and intrusion, and those which offer choice, and genuine wisdom. But with their propensity towards trance, and their opening out of consciousness beyond the personal psyche, they may come into life with the specific purpose of allowing themselves to be taken over by the astral dimension, and fall victim to it. This was not uncommon with shamans in the past. They often remained in a 'dismembered' or psychologically disintegrated state throughout their lives. Although personally and socially incapacitated, they were still responsive to the strong demands of the tribe, and could bring through healing, wisdom and help. But, in a sense, they were victims of the tribe.

Today the person experiencing mental illness may be not so much the victim of the tribe, for they are not compelled to perform shamanically. But they have often chosen at a very deep level to sacrifice the personality in this incarnation to the greater well being of society at large. Their 'person' becomes a vehicle through which lower astral energies are discharged, earthed, and diffused during their lifetime, while their incarnating spirit has to a large extent withdrawn. In many ways, they resemble the incapacitated tribal shaman of the past, except that, today, Western society does not recognize the shaman's role in society, or that even an incapacitated shaman can fulfill a helping, healing role in the community. Without the social context for the shaman in your culture, the person suffering mental illness can only silently fulfill their unacknowledged purpose. They become a 'conductor of chaos,' discharging the residues, sometimes from aeons of human life, which have become trapped in the wider spiritual body of humanity, and not simply within the individual. And, as we shall see, these residues need to be sounded out—expressed—and then grounded upon this planet of music and healing.

The purging of spirit

While acting as a 'conductor of chaos' on behalf of the wider community is one important, unacknowledged aspect of much mental illness, there is also another, deeply intimate process going on, which is specific to the individual's own spiritual growth.

As it evolves, the spirit constructs a soul-body of greater and greater refinement and light. For many people—for many spirits, if you like—there are areas within their wider field of spirit which need to be balanced, and brought more in tune with the essentially well-balanced, well-tuned, and refined frequency on which they live. Often when a person experiences mental illness, they are going through a kind of purging of those aspects of their own wider field of spirit, which are preventing it from being more balanced and fully integrated.

The beginning of this purging process is when that spirit incarnates into physical life. Initially they may be 'all there' in terms of their self-consciousness. The spirit is present. But this particular kind of incarnation goes on to become another form of 'self' sacrifice, for the spirit needs to 'sacrifice' — literally to 'make sacred' — that discordant aspect of its overall, wider field, which is preventing it from being more whole. That discordant complex is expressed through the suffering of the soul, and through the mentally disturbed personality, which are then sacrificed to physical life.

In much mental illness, it often seems as if a person's spirit has left and deserted them. And it is true the spirit *does* withdraw from incarnation to a large extent. It moves back closer to the dimension of existence from which it has come, and where its 'larger self' always is. It leaves behind the personality, and the incarnated soul, still embodied and going through the agony of mental illness. That person becomes like a ghost to their former self, and indeed this is what they are in a certain sense. They are like an embodied ghost, for they need to remain in physical life in order to diffuse, discharge, and discard the discordant energies which can no longer be blended or integrated with their larger, spiritual self. These energies may either be those trapped pockets of negativity from the collective, which the individual has 'taken on,' or they may have arisen from more 'personal karma' over a number of lives. Either way, the need to restore balance within the larger field of their spirit leads to this purging, through which the soul experiences abandonment.

An abandoned soul

So there is this element of real sacrifice going through much mental illness. Having been brought into incarnation, the soul remains there with the body, even though the spirit has withdrawn. It is literally 'dispirited,' and has, in a sense, been deserted. It is as if part of the agony of mental illness is the soul crying out to the spirit — rather like Jesus on the cross crying out to God — 'Why have you deserted me?' For that person feels abandoned by their spirit. They are still obliged to go through the motions of living, but do so, in a sense, 'rudderless' — without the guidance of their spirit, which normally brings a sense of direction, integrity, and presence.

It is as if the person suffering this kind of mental illness is living through a dream, or rather a nightmare, one of abandonment and this tragic sense of desertion. They incarnated into conditions which prevented their spirit from growing. It was blocked by the very circumstances it chose to incarnate into. So the spirit partially withdrew, leaving the soul in many ways stranded. One of the great tragedies of mental illness is the perception and experience of a person who is still a sentient soul, but whose spirit appears to have withdrawn, and indeed, to some extent, *has* withdrawn.

In cases where people recover from mental illness, there may be a different 'agenda' for the spirit. It is as if they have to go through that experience of incarnating, then withdrawing, and then almost like reincarnating within the same lifetime, in order for that purging and refining to take place through this form of soul suffering. For it is the soul that suffers; the spirit does not suffer in such a deeply physical way, having withdrawn.

Treating mental illness

With the understanding that certain forms of mental illness involve a person discharging both individual and collective residues of blocked energy, there are things which can be done to assist them. The first thing is for other people's perception and understanding of what is happening to change. For this can have actual practical consequences. In a way, part of the treatment is the change in outlook of other members of society upon what is happening, so that these people are approached with compassion. Instead of turning its back upon the mentally ill, society needs to turn more towards them and give help, both in containing their experience and in diffusing their energies. Much of the fear and rejection of the mentally ill in your society is to do with the failure to understand what their experience is about, of what they are going through, and why they are going through it.

Secondly, the experiences of the person suffering mental illness need to be acknowledged as real for them, for they are real. The astral worlds have their own reality, which may seem unreal, like a fantasy, to those immersed in physical life. But those very same forces which are being rejected as unreal are the ones which underpin the drama of every single person's life on Earth, except that they do not rock the boat in the same way, or capsize it. The ship at sea analogy is actually a very helpful one in this case. At sea, when a boat is struggling or sinking, it is normal for other ships to come to its assistance, not to turn away, not to sail off in the other direction; instinctively, they seek to support and maybe save those who are sinking or drowning.

There needs to be a huge turn-around in your society towards the awareness that many individuals suffering mental illness are carrying out a particular form of incarnation, discharging, or cleansing the collective psyche, enabling it to maintain a certain balance and equilibrium; and that perhaps they are sharing with their family this process of cathartic rebalancing, which reverberates out, affecting not only the whole of humanity, but indeed the whole universe.

Calling upon Earth's spirit

Now there are many mentally ill people who are not carrying out this process within the context of the family group. They seem to be totally isolated and on their own. The experience of mental illness often drives other people away, leaving that person utterly withdrawn and abandoned, often resistant and unresponsive to conventional treatment. They just seem to live a vegetative life, as if dead within. It is as if they are in an endless limbo state, trapped, beyond help, abandoned, as we have already seen, not only by others, but also by their very own spirit. They are souls in hell. What can be done for them?

As your spirit, or an aspect of your spirit, incarnates into physical life on Earth, it picks up with Earth's spirit, with that incarnational force of the power animal, which binds you to life on Earth. As it enters Earth's aura, your spirit gathers momentum, the momentum of the magnetic pull to keep you here. It is engaging with Earth's spirit, as manifest or expressed through your own elemental spirit, or power animal. This intelligent force breathes physical life into you and is aware of the purpose of your incarnation. It draws close to you and enters your field of experience as you move more deeply into life on Earth and are embodied here.

Now it is important to realize that *the* spirit—your own essence—can live, move, and have its being, in many different realms, anywhere in the universe it chooses. But it chooses to incarnate on Earth for a specific purpose. And through that process of incarnation, it engages with the energy of what we are calling the power animal, which binds you to life on Earth. Obviously, *the* spirit—your own essence—is not the same as your power animal, which is specific to life on Earth. And even when a person's essential self, or spirit, withdraws, as in some forms of mental illness, the elemental energy of their power animal is still available to them. Even if the purpose of that incarnation is for *the* spirit to withdraw back into its wider field, the energy of the power animal remains accessible to that person at the level of Earth life.

So where is this leading? It is leading to the notion that one way of helping people who are suffering mental illness—who have been deserted by their spirit—is to summon up and draw upon the vitality of their power animal. For it is still binding them to Earth. So long as they are alive, that spirit is accessible to them. Clearly, in many cases, this energy also appears to have withdrawn to a large extent, for the person may desperately lack vitality. But it is still available. As we have already seen with certain degenerative diseases, *sound* may be used for healing dis-ease. In this case, it may be used to summon the power animal. Its energies may literally be *called upon*. For, once again, with Earth being the planet of sound and healing, if a person *calls*, or is helped to summon up that elemental spirit, which belongs to them, it can be sounded out and asked to enter more deeply into their being. Even if they are going to spend the rest of this particular life to some extent abandoned by their own essential self, they can still be nurtured by Earth's spirit. They may be leading dispirited lives, lacking the sense of direction which comes from the presence of their own spirit. But if they can be helped to find *that sound* within themselves, which will call up the energies of their power animal, and make it a more constant presence, they may be able to experience much more vitality and animation, and enter into life on Earth more fully. The incarnational energy of the power animal will not necessarily give them a sense of direction but it may give them a much deeper experience of the nurturing, healing presence of Earth's spirit, and help them to discharge those discordant energies effectively, as part of their life's task.

This greater Earth connection for the person suffering mental illness may bring about a quicker resolution of their task; and they may also find a degree of comfort in their lives through that elemental support. This is why, for many mentally ill patients, activities like gardening and relationships with animals can be tremendously nurturing. In those areas they are more directly in touch with Earth's spirit, without having to negotiate through the intellect of other people, and their preconceptions. Similarly, experiences with the sea, or with dolphins, as in the case of autistic children, for example, have already proved to have tremendously healing effects. For they are in direct contact with Earth's healing spirit of water and the unconditional love, expressed through these beings.

A vision for the future

Even though mental illness may seem very complex, it may be viewed more simply as a case where the spirit has to some extent been ousted by shadow energies from the astral dimension. At a deeper level, the spirit may be understood to have withdrawn more willingly. These shadow energies have for a long time dominated the larger part of the human physical body, causing disease. In the case of some mental illness, it is as if this tide of astral energies has risen above the head and submerged brain consciousness. Today, instead of swimming largely within those astral waters, the potential is there for humankind, both individually and collectively, to step out of this sea of emotion and dry out. As you move away from the dominance by largely astral forces, your whole body may become the container of these energies, rather than being so deeply immersed in them. As this happens, mental illness will become less and less prevalent in the future.

Just as mental illness will be less prevalent in the future, so will there also be less and less need for the shaman of the past, who left the physical body in order to enter the astral worlds. With this transformation taking place in the focus and orientation of human awareness, the potential is there to shift more deeply into the physical body, rather than wrenching consciousness away from it. As you move out of an age of the emotions into an age of thought, the mind will align itself right down the whole physical body into all the cells, and thought will become the ambience of experience. As it does so, then the emotions—that powerful sea of astral experience—will be a rich source of experience in human life, both of joy, and maybe sometimes sorrow. But it will no longer be so dominant.

As the ice age of the spirit comes to an end, human consciousness will be realigned into its rightful position, gently embedded within physical life on Earth. This is a vision for the future. Meanwhile those with mental illness continue to suffer; and for them, they can be helped simply by other people understanding what is happening to them.

CHAPTER 15

FREEDOM OF SPIRIT

You seek the final pearl of this saga. A pearl is the refinement of much experience, the solid end-product of a long process of distilling, refining, and digesting — of working through the materials in the world, and allowing spirit to act upon them. That pearl is rather like the shining soul-body of light.

Finding your own true rhythm

Freedom of spirit is about allowing your essence, or true self, to express itself at every moment, in whatever way, at its own true rhythm. Slavery is the spirit bound to manifest at a rhythm which does not suit it. There are circumstances which allow the spirit to grow in incarnation; and there are circumstances which seem to block this growth. But the more fully you allow your being — the vibration of your own being — to enter deeply into physical life, the more it creates and manifests its own field *at that level of existence*; and as it does so, it generates the circumstances which it needs for its growth.

Your experience of freedom will become more and more palpable, the more you move away from what you believe is expected from you in the world. That is freedom, for you are no longer slave to the structures of your culture, but are able to move through them and with them in your own way. You may dance with them, but you are not chained by them.

You, as an energy, or spirit, are traveling a path; and only you can travel that path. There is *no way* that you can experience life for any other person, or prescribe what is right or wrong for them. This has caused so much grief to the whole of humanity — this attempt to lay down the path which others should tread as being right or wrong for them. It is the most damaging, crippling grip which one human being can try to keep on another. Ultimately, no matter how things appear on the surface, one person, one soul, one spirit, cannot hold another in their grip. It can only appear so, the nearer you are to the level of action in the physical world. There is, of course, collusion between people at a deep, unconscious level about the roles they will enact with each other during their lives on Earth. But the fact of this collusion—or subtle agreement—should not let the attempt to grip, hold, and manipulate each other's lives go unchallenged. It needs to be brought up and exposed. For the more it is laid bare and understood, the less people will go on perpetuating the need to manipulate each other and be manipulated, to be victims and victimizers.

The attempt to grip and manipulate another person distorts your own energy, channeling it away from far more creative expressions of life. The energy is not wasted, because energy is never wasted. But it is channeled down paths which do not lead to the flowering and growth of your potential.

For many, many people—perhaps even for the majority of humanity—feeling 'not free' has been, and still is a dominant characteristic of their lives on Earth. It perpetuates itself when the enslaved individual tries to control and enslave others and prevent *them* from being free. And there is no real answer to this dilemma today at the purely human level. One can fight, and campaign, and work to help free people from various forms of bondage or slavery in the world. But the real move towards greater freedom will be when people move beyond the need to exercise unwarranted influence on the path of another person's life. Making laws to prevent abuse is only treating the symptoms. It does not treat the real cause of why one person should wish to enslave another, and why the enslaved person, in many ways, at a certain deep level, is prepared to be enslaved, why they are prepared to give up their own power to another.

So there is only a limited amount which can be done through the structures of your culture to create conditions for greater freedom. To find the 'root'—literally the 'root' as in a plant, and also the 'route' as the path towards this greater freedom—you need to approach and enter that finer frequency of your being, where the experience of your many lives has accumulated, where it has become refined and concentrated as a source of knowledge and wisdom. It is in this 'space' that your spirit is already free, yet seeks greater freedom for you at the level of your life on Earth, where you are right now. It moves you to find the understanding which brings greater freedom and peace.

This is your life

Freedom of spirit is being able to walk away from a situation if you feel you no longer need it, and it is being able to stay in a situation which you feel you still need for your growth. Freedom of spirit is especially being able to move on when the time has come to move on.

While these are expressions of individual freedom, what about the culture you belong to, which you obviously cannot just walk away from? How do you experience freedom of spirit within the bounds of that culture? Firstly, by not trying to change it, deliberately, consciously. Accept where you are. Be where you are, for change will only come through that deeper incarnation of your own spirit, of that frequency which is uniquely yours. Don't *try*. You don't need to try and do anything. Work from where you are, from your center, and in your own way transform your culture as it expresses itself at that point where you are.

You belong to your culture, and are as much part of it as anyone else 'out there.' In many ways, the distinction between 'here' and 'out there' is arbitrary and false. It is exaggerated by your media, as if what is *really* going on is 'out there,' in the news, or wherever. But there is no 'out there.' There is only where you are. Taking too seriously much of what you read and hear expressed through the media, and through politicians, is a very, very large distraction. For it supports the belief that your circumstances come first, and *you* come second, that money, work, houses, lives—even your life—are more important than your own being, your consciousness.

Try to be clear about where your life begins and ends. For in a certain important sense, the parameters of your life are different to those of your consciousness. Ultimately your consciousness can reach out to every other human spirit, in or out of incarnation, because you yourself belong to the body of humanity. Your consciousness could expand to be at one with the whole consciousness of the human race, and even beyond into the wider universe. But this is not the same as where your life begins and ends, or of having the clarity to be able to say, 'This is my life, this is not my life.' What you wish to introduce into your life and what you do not—*this* is where you have choice and where your freedom lies.

There is a difference in quality between your consciousness and your life. Your consciousness exists largely out of time, whereas your life takes place, and is enacted, in time. Only an aspect of your spirit enters into the flow of time. Understanding that your own being and consciousness extend beyond the beginning and the end of your life can help you enter into it more deeply and wholeheartedly. In a sense, your life is something you can hold in your hand. It is finite, whereas your being and consciousness are not. They are eternal.

Freedom of spirit is to do with entering more deeply into the physicality of your life, bringing into it that sense of a more natural rhythm. It is about bringing your life and consciousness closer together, so that time merges with timelessness, and the line of time is no longer dominant. You know yourself to be part of that eternal stream of consciousness upon which you are totally dependent. In this sense, you cannot 'be,' and *not be* dependent. For who and what you are only becomes who and what you are as an offshoot of the source from which all life, in all universes, is generated. Just as you are dependent upon that source of all life, so you *are* also that source of all life. If you can contain that understanding within your own mind, that understanding of your utter dependence, and also your utter ultimate identification with the source of life itself, which permeates every atom and molecule of creation, then rather than needing to be free, you can 'just be.'

Dependent upon Earth

Freedom of spirit enables you to accept your dependence upon Earth, so long as you are within its realm, paradoxical as this may seem. Everyone who is born on Earth to some extent goes through a degree of dependency, not only upon their physical, biological mother, but also upon that far deeper, more archetypal energy — of Earth. An incarnation into Earth, in a physical sense, is incarnation into a dependent relationship. That is what it's about. There is no getting away from that. Since you are born physically, for as long as you are alive on Earth, you are dependent upon Earth.

Although many people, as spirits, need to come into Earth to experience life as this level, a certain part of that spirit may sometimes resent giving up the greater mobility and freedom they have when outside of a physical body. A lot of that resentment comes through previous experiences of not having fully incarnated. For when you are not fully incarnate you are profoundly aware, both of the pull towards Earth and away from it, instead of allowing yourself to be gently drawn deeply into that experience. So long as you try to resist that pull, you resent it. So long as you see yourself separate from that source of nourishment, you are always going to experience yourself as if you are the child, the dependent child, rather than also as the source of nourishment yourself.

In other words, until you can be both mother and child at once, at the same time dependent and also nurturing, you are going to continue feeling pulled between these polarized extremes of experience. You are not alone in this, for it is an archetypal experience running through the whole of humanity. It is a fundamental human experience, the whole issue of wanting to be independent, yet feeling and being dependent. Many religions have tried to avoid this dependence upon Earth, adopting a posture of arrogance and aloofness out fear of Earth's spirit — fear of letting go and being just like any other form of creation on Earth, mutually interdependent. This arrogance has alienated the spirits in other kingdoms of nature, which often fear human beings, just as they themselves are feared by humans. The very spirit of vitality which human beings have as their fundamental inheritance from being upon Earth — what we are calling the spirit of shamanism — has been denigrated and repressed. For the ancient Greeks it manifested as the god, Pan, later becoming the devil in Christianity, as Earth's spirit was pushed further away from the natural experience into which every person is born.

Freedom from slavery

Slavery is the spirit incarnating into circumstances which prevent it from vibrating at its own frequency. It is slave to the conditions into which it is incarnating. This happens because that spirit has not fully incarnated. For with its full incarnation, it transforms life around it. It creates or finds what it needs — in order to 'be.' Just as you find true power when power is genuinely of no more concern for you, so you find freedom when freedom is no longer of any concern to you, when life just 'is,' and you just 'are.'

When the spirit is dominated by the analytical mind, it dissects life, generating polarities and extremes of experience. These in turn create tensions and contradictions, which block the spirit's fuller incarnation. In a sense, deeper incarnation of spirit and freedom of spirit, are the same thing. They both require the quietening of that intellectual aspect of your mind, which is so often out-of-balance and out-of-sync with the rest of your being; it is judging, condemning, criticizing, and generating tension and conflict. You can be a far more potent force for change in your world by realizing how criticism, judgement and condemnation feed the very thing which you are criticizing, the very thing which seems so wrong to you. It breathes life into it. This is where human folly lies — in not understanding how you *fuel* with your own negativity the very conditions which seem to block you, enabling these obstacles to grow out of all proportion. Something which seems so wrong to you can be most easily deflated by your willingness not to fuel it, by not being compelled to feed it. This also means not feeding it silently within your own mind. It is not simply a matter of not expressing negativity. Many people, especially within the Christian tradition, do not say critical words out loud to others because they have been taught that it is 'wrong' to do so. But they are often thinking them in their minds. Absence of judgement is not the same as quietly harboring critical thoughts. It is genuinely being able to look at those thoughts face on, the moment they fly into your psychic space, and then let go of them.

So freedom of spirit, in a way, is about learning to be better and better housekeepers of your own psychic space, of being prepared to say 'Yes, I'm letting this in. No, I'm not keeping that.' For what you let in and keep becomes *yours*, and *is* yours. It is what 'being yours' is about—belonging to you and your own unique experience. Freedom of spirit is about learning to exercise this choice, not only of what comes your way, but also of what actually remains part of you. If something which you don't like seems to be part of you, you learn not to feed it. You just let it be. Maybe you just need to accept that it's there. But you don't criticize, judge, and condemn yourself because it is there. Perhaps you find that you are greedy, or needy, or dependent; or you want others to be dependent upon you and to need you. Perhaps this is part of you. But if you fuel it with passion, and feed it with criticism, judgement, and condemnation, with all those powerful astral forces, they will take a hold of your being and enslave you. Your *acknowledgement* of something within your own being, which you may not like, is a far more potent force for freedom of spirit than trying to exorcise your psychic space and make it an empty space. That spiritual quest for deep, empty space really reflects the need to accept what you find within yourself. But you do not have to get tense about it. You are relaxed.

Trusting your pulse
Individually, freedom of spirit is very much about finding what gives you 'zest,' what makes you love doing what you are doing, no matter how, or where, or with whom you are doing it. If you trust your spirit, and if you trust your own soul or psyche, your psyche will bring forth the conditions it needs for its own growth. In a sense, trusting your psyche is the precondition for freedom of spirit, and for freedom from slavery. As a plant seeks the light, so

your psyche seeks out the conditions it needs to grow. The less you block it with your preconceptions of what you should be doing, the more it will find those conditions. For psyche is not purely mythic, it is also organic — 'she' is also organic. She is the nymph. She is soul, she moves with the energies of Earth when allowed to. She is a natural manifestation.

Feel your pulse. Trust your own heartbeat as your guide — it is right there with you every moment. Allow your body to be your guide — your 'power animal,' in that true and deep sense of being your most tangible guide with a wisdom of its own, its own savvy knowledge of life on Earth. Your physical body is your own Earth spirit guide. Instead of seeking direction and answers in terms of concepts and thoughts, allow yourself to be moved and taught through the images, impulses and directions of your own body, as well as those coming from Earth itself — by the movements of the clouds, by the wind whispering, by the trees rustling. For they are all speaking to each other, and to you. Your pains, judgements, criticisms, and condemnations, are very human. But freedom of spirit is also the freedom to be able to engage with the many other non-human forms of life around you in a real way. You come to realize that they have 'insides' like you do; and just as you are aware of the interior of the life within you, so you become aware of the interior of Earth's life, Earth's organic imagination, which surrounds and supports you. This is not so much about what you need to *do*, as about finding the rhythm of your being and your life, finding a settled relationship with that rhythm, and *allowing it to reach out to the rhythm of Earth's spirit*. For that is where freedom of spirit lies.

Earth's time
And so we come to the key to this whole question, to the root of the problem, which has kept you, as a human being, from your full immersion in the living spirit of Earth, as an aspect of your overall experience and evolution, for you are a being on a journey which takes you through many forms of experience. These experiences refine the substance of your being, extending, expanding, broad-

ening the field of your spirit. Eventually you reach the finest frequency of life, where, as the source of life itself, you enter into every aspect of creation in all universes.

Now this is not some great fantasy but a fact of existence — it is where you already are. You are a conscious aspect of the source of life, experiencing itself through the medium of physical life on Earth. But so long as you understand yourself to be *only* an aspect, to be limited, this sense of limitation instills and engenders the quest and thirst for freedom. The more wholeheartedly you enter into your experience in any realm, the more you bring through that refinement and power of your extended self, and ultimately of the source of life itself.

Just as the spirit of Earth comes to meet you, as you incarnate and enter into its sphere of life, so in coming to meet Earth, you bring your eternal self. This is what all those notions of 'Heaven on Earth' are about — the human being bringing fully and deeply into incarnation their spirit which exists in eternal time. No longer drawn or pulled away, or dragged down, it enters gently into time, bringing timelessness into that experience. It enters into the natural rhythms and cycles of Earth's being, into Earth's time, feeling the rhythm and pulse of organic existence.

In creating your own artificial time, you paralyze that ability to enter into the natural rhythm of Earth's tempo, and to be at one with it. For there is an echo of eternity in Earth's time, in the cycles of its time, which is absent in your line of time. In Earth's time, forms may have a beginning and an ending, but they blend into each other, coming in and out of existence, in their own natural way. They manifest and then withdraw, just as you manifest and then withdraw, as part of a natural organic process.

You can experience freedom within Earth's time — in the beauty of each season with its own quality, its own characteristics, which give form and color to all the manifestations of life around you. This is Earth's soul speaking and expressing itself, and you are partaking of that soul, for you belong to Earth's soul, so long as you are incarnate on Earth.

Each aspect of nature presents itself in its own right, each has its own being. Yet it presents itself in a form which is mutually balanced, and interactive with the other forms of life around it. There is this symbiosis of relationship throughout the whole of the natural world. And it is through this interaction with all other forms of life that you enter into Earth's time, and there you may experience more deeply and more fully your own spirit in incarnation, as part of the whole rather than isolated from it. You are no longer living your life on a conveyor belt with the seconds ticking away. You are living within each aspect of the cycle of time, in Earth's time, within that space or 'place' which is called 'autumn,' within that 'place' which is called 'winter.' For each of the seasons generates itself as a location within Earth's realm, as a pulse within the rhythm of Earth's breath, and heartbeat. Each season is an expression of an eternal quality within Earth's time. When you enter into and move through the seasons as if they were locations of Earth's spirit, then you enter eternal time.

Do you want to be someone remembered in your culture? Do want success within the artificial structures and hierarchies of your civilization, which lasts just for a moment? Or do your want your own unique place within that deeply embedded, eternal time of Earth's cycles, and to drink fully of your experience here, bringing the expression of your own eternal spirit into those cycles of Earth's time? As it evolves, your spirit may need to move on into other realms of experience. This is all the more reason to nurture your own dependence upon Earth, not to mind it, but to love it — to love being on Earth, and of Earth, and with Earth's spirit, to love walking through the temples of its seasons.

Earth's time is sacred. The seasons are the rooms in Earth's temple — the spaces within which you may walk in the eternal 'now.' They are literally expressions of Heaven in Earth, in Earth's being, 'Heaven' in the sense of being infinite spaces manifesting in the finite, of being eternal rhythms expressing themselves in the temporal.

You are as much a part of Earth's spirit as the hills, and the trees, and the rivers, the winds, the animals, every form which partakes of life belongs to Earth's spirit. Humanity is not tacked on to it, nor is Earth is a space ship, and you the space-travelers. Earth is a living being. To the extent that you belong to Earth's being, you *are* Earth's being.

The marriage of Heaven and Earth

You may think that Earth could survive happily without human beings. But your existence as part of Earth's being is essential for the evolution of this great spirit. Part of you, what we are calling 'the power animal,' your elemental self, is integral to this planet, and always belongs to Earth. Your freedom of spirit during your life on Earth is very much determined by your relationship with this elemental spirit, and by knowing that you can always call upon it. It is through this relationship that you may enter into nature and experience it 'inside out.' All around you, and also within your own physical being, is Earth's organic imagination. The organic imagination of Earth's spirit expresses itself physically and locally as your own body, through the cells, the nerves, the bones, the forms of your own body; and these were not constructed from nowhere. They were created out of that marriage of your eternal spirit with Earth's spirit, through that unique relationship with your power animal, bringing you into being, giving you physical substance, knowing the purpose of your life. It is your intimate contact, as spirit, with the substance and spirit of Earth.

Cherish the sublime intimacy of this experience you are going through — *now* — in your life on Earth. As the marriage of Heaven and Earth, it is sacred, and uniquely yours.

CONCLUSION

The shaman has always been the center of tribal life, in the sense of being the spiritual focus or 'hearth' of the tribe. There have of course been times when they have lived a marginal life on the edge of society. But, still, members of the tribe would seek out the shaman to access what they understood to be the living stream of consciousness from beyond the mundane—to bring it through into daily life. In many cases, the shaman would actively *seek out* the sources of wisdom, understanding, and knowledge from the 'worlds beyond.' In other cases, the spirits would *come to* them without their needing to leave the physical body. And while definitions may attempt to pin down who or what a shaman is, in essence their role has been to maintain the deepest possible contact with the source of life, in whatever culture they have lived.

Against the backdrop of the last ice age, the shaman did embody, or manifest, the hidden spirit of a frozen Earth at a particular time when the planet was going through its initiation by ice. At that time there was a desperate, essential need for the individual who could express the intrinsic warmth, life and joy of Earth's spirit, whilst these life-giving energies were being eclipsed by the ice. This spirit of the shaman—and of shamanism—has survived until today. It cannot *not* survive, for, at its deepest level, it represents the ability of humanity to live on Earth, and with Earth's spirit. There is a symbiosis between human evolution and Earth's evolution. Both are closely linked in with each other, even though Earth's evolution has its own awesome time span. But what was once the sole preserve of this gifted individual—the shaman—in tribal societies is now an emerging collective awareness of that essential, elemental, vital life, which courses through the nerves, cells and blood vessels of every human being incarnate on the planet, as well as through every other aspect of life on Earth.

The difference between the shaman of the past and the shaman of today is that, in the past, the shaman first separated from the tribe and then returned to it in order to bring help and healing. Today the Western mind as a whole has been separated from 'the tribe,' in the sense that it has been set apart and alienated from itself. This experience of an existential wilderness has been running through the whole of modern life. As the spirit of shamanism resurfaces within the collective psyche, it brings back a sense of the communal hearth around which every member of the human tribe sits, and is warmed. This sense of the hearth allows the experience of all people, and all forms of life, to be seen and understood as equally valid as each other. There is an acceptance that each person's path through life is unique yet at the same time a completely, totally valid aspect of our whole, global culture.

Courage and acceptance
The shaman today — the 'new shaman' — is not one who needs to set him- or herself above others, or as distinct from others, or as especially eccentric or different. They do not have to emphasize their uniqueness because they know that it is implicit in their being. But what they can do is bring with them that *courage* needed to acknowledge and accept every other form of experience as being equally valid. Just as one great talent of the shaman in the past has been to search for and bring back lost souls, so their gift today is to bring an acceptance of the *story* of each soul. For what is the value of bringing back souls, if you then judge, criticize and condemn the tale they have to tell, the path that they have been along?

The new shaman does not need to preach, or to convert people, because for them each unique spark of life — each person — vibrates and radiates their own cellular frequency into the teeming physical world. It requires no effort. It is a physical fact of life that everyone is made of the same 'stuff,' the stuff which is, in a sense, on loan to the individual from the universe for the purpose of experience. Everyone shares this same 'borrowing' of the energy needed to experience life — no one is exempt. But what each person makes of it is an expression of their own unique, vital essence which makes them different to any other aspect of creation. Each spark of life creates the diversity and variety of the myriad forms of experience. Nothing, no one is the same; no experience can be the same from one moment to the next.

Finding the middle way
Looking ahead to the future, there is often the feeling that things will go on being same as they are in the present. In other words, through repetition, those deeply ingrained patterns or rhythms of the past will not be able to raise themselves to the next octave of life in the future. Instead of the next turn on the spiral, things simply seem to go round and round in circles. The energy or spirit of shamanism is an uplifting force, making consciousness lighter and raising experience to a level where it is possible to breathe out that sense of being stuck in the past. It is radical. In lifting the spirit, in lightening experience, it is not denying the dark, the shadow. The shadow, the dark, is faced and acknowledged. It is seen for what it is, but it is not the determining factor. It is more like a counter-force or balance.

The life of any human being, of any individual, is always fluctuating between the pull towards life and the pull away from it. There has been a massive, negative surge through the consciousness and awareness of the human race to pull or draw away and reject your Earth incarnation, at the same time as being impelled to come here for experience. This conflict is part of what stimulates consciousness. But it has become so fraught that it has paralyzed consciousness. The pull away has been too great and forced its polar opposite — the pull towards Earth — to be too great as well, whereas incarnation could be far gentler. So both tendencies have become too extreme.

With the shift in the orientation towards the spiritual hearth, towards a greater caring, loving sense of communal life, and with the struggle into birth of the truly global village, humanity can more gently plant the seed of consciousness within the substance of Earth without feeling so shot away, or dragged and pulled down into it. There will be much more gentleness and a greater sense of choice; and, again, this is where the shaman comes in. The truly empowered shaman in the past has experienced these extremes and found ways to bridge them, while the dismembered, disempowered shaman has become victim of these forces. The new shaman will acknowledge these polarized energies and seek the middle way towards helping people gently lay down their personal burdens which seem to cripple their lives. This does not mean to say that there will be no personal life. It simply means that the effect of the shadow in one's life will no longer be so overwhelming and paralyzing. Instead it will be there as night is in relation to day, not as a dominant experience, with fear being the ruling force.

Perhaps if you find yourself hurting because of the issues you have brought into this life, which were stirred up during the early part of your life here, and you wonder 'Is this pain never going to go away?' then look into the life of the creatures around you. You will sense and notice that only those who live close to human beings seem, perhaps, to retain the memory of their trauma as a high point in their being, as a prominent feature, as something which is maintained as a focus. Most, however, let their experiences become eroded and changed by their inner tides and winds, by their inner landscape, their inner nature. It is all consigned to the same larger process of natural movement and change. *They don't make a monument of their suffering.* Whereas you not only make a monument of it, you often compete with each other to see who's monument is bigger, larger, more deserving of attention. So much can be learned through your friends or cousins of other species, especially your relatives in the plant and tree worlds. They may hold a memory of suffering but it will not be the prominent feature of their being and of their experience. The difference is that they will not repress their anguish at the moment of the trauma. They will express it and then move on. With the powerful grip of the human mind, you hold and delay your expressions, so that they seem to override your experience, and your own being.

The fire and joy of the spirit
The new shaman will learn to stand close up against fear, but not within the aura, as it were, of fear. They may experience fear, but not in a way that dominates and drives their life. There will be a crossing of that bridge between what seem to be two very distinct ways of living, one within fear, one beyond fear, one unfulfilled,

the other fulfilled, one joyless, the other full of joy. There is absolutely no sense in which an individual must condemn themselves to a life of joylessness. They may have brought with them many factors which predispose them towards a difficult life, and many opportunities for pain. But this does not mean that their lives have to be eclipsed by these experiences, or that their essential flame has to be snuffed out by them.

Hold on to whatever you find in your life which gives you, even for a moment, a sense of personal enjoyment, a momentary sense of that joy which springs from a natural interplay between you and whatever it is that you are enjoying. It is that play, that gift of delight springing up—*that* is the life and the spirit which runs through your being, as a being in relation to Earth. It is something you share with all forms of life and can see in the play of the young of other species. Kindle that spirit when you sense it. Take hold of it.

The terrain in which people can open out and extend themselves to the joy and the play of life is always available. It is always there, but often forgotten. The senses in the soles of your feet, which can let in that spirit directly, have become numb. All you need to do is to feel it, through your hands, through your feet, through your physical body, to experience that feeling of life. Yes, you often get caught up in the negative, in the dark, miserable, critical and judgmental; and without all that you wouldn't be able to fully comprehend your greater wholeness. You need that experience, but only for the twinkling of an eye. It is only for a moment that you need to forget, so that you can remember again. And in that remembering you will have grown beyond the horizon of where you stood before, in fuller consciousness.

Each time you turn towards the grayness of human life, those areas where the warmth has faded, let the sun return just by 'being there,' because you contain that sun. There is no need to be dismayed by what you perceive, for you carry so much more within you than you know. This is what the shaman has always done—to enter in to that whole vast world of 'more-than-you-could-ever-think-that-you-knew.' It is a world of experience, not simply knowledge. It's not second-hand knowledge. It doesn't need books or book learning.

When you see around you what appears to be a world full of suffering and pain inflicted by one upon another, a world of injustice, there is always a desire to improve life. But how? 'How?' — you may say — 'I am overwhelmed by so much misery and suffering. I don't know where to start. I feel paralyzed by it all.' Try to remember that everything you bring into your awareness does not need to be acted upon in the physical world. It helps to understand the issues in the world, for understanding is an act in itself. But it does not require action in time and through space. If you try to deal with the ills of the world at the level at which you perceive them, you become an ill of the world yourself. If you offer your perception of the world, perhaps, in a sense, as a sacrifice, consigning it to *the fire of your spirit*, then in that very little act, that tiny gesture, you are not only disposing of it from your psyche, you are allowing it to be spiritualized. It is being moved into a finer frequency where the potential for its transformation is far greater.

You may think that consigning the world's problems to an inner fire seems to be quite a callous type of move — you are not suffering enough yourself. But you don't need to suffer. There is already enough suffering in the world. In that tiny little act, using your perception of pain to kindle your own inner fire, the fire of your spirit, you are allowing this spiritual energy to use it to produce the heat needed for healing in the world. That is *all* you need to do. And unless you feel called to a particular area where you can be effective in helping other people, then you will be doing an enormous amount by recycling your perception of the world, your perception of the pain, through your spirit, without having to suffer.

So enter your new terrain, your new ground. Humankind has been through many, many, many incarnations where there has been so much pain, the pain of forgetting, and the struggle to remember. You are not in exile. You are at home at whatever moment you choose to remember your home. Wherever you are is where you belong.

APPENDIXES

Author's Note

After completing this book, I still felt that the story of the origins of shamanism told in Part I needed to unfold further and that some deeper insights were waiting in the wings, as it were, to be presented on stage. Having experienced such a strong affinity with Paleolithic shamanism, especially the cave paintings and engravings, I decided to tune in to this inner resonance and carry out inner work in order to seek answers to a number of questions. The first concerned the extraordinary fact that 'anatomically modern humans'—people looking and to some extent behaving like us—have been present on Earth for an incredibly short time, perhaps between 100,000 and 150,000 years, less than the blink of an eye in the evolution of Earth's life. So our appearance seems to have been quite sudden and remains a riddle to mainstream science.

Another question concerned our ancestors' relationship with their Neanderthal cousins. I felt that there was more to understand about their 'communion of consciousness,' which needed to be explored.

Finally, from Chapter 1, I wanted to know what that inspirational force was—the "great Upper Paleolithic *daimon*"—which animated our ice-age ancestors into such vigorous and mystical, creative activity. These two final sections offer the results of further channeled research.

Appendix 1 to Chapters 2 and 3

"You seek an image or a picture to give you more clarity in your quest to understand the origins of people like yourself. The scientific search for these answers has been obscured—confounded, if you like—by shadow energies which have created confusion, polarities, conflicts; and despite this, your scientists have managed to create a story of Earth's life which inspires awe for the sheer magnitude of the length of its life and the transformations Earth has gone through. But so long as science overlooks the spirit, it will remain in ignorance of the purpose of Earth's life, and of the origins and purpose of human life.

In the beginning, it was as if the various different kinds of life were to be seeded upon Earth as it evolved. For Earth lived a life almost out of time during its early evolution. It was not fully incarnate, which is why so much of its early history is inaccessible. But there have been many phases and stages of growth of this planet, and many of these were linked to the energies of other planets in the solar system, in the same way that members of a family are linked to each other and grow together.

Now, the arrival of human life took place through a process of spirit incarnating into the bodies of those early humans which your scientists have discovered. What they have not discovered is the intelligence and humanity of these people, even beyond the time of the last ice age, and way back into the beginning, near to the beginning of the whole cycle of the ice epoch. Humanity has evolved on Earth in order to understand and experience love physically, and this has been going on for millions of years. However, Earth became subjected to great waves of negativity, which has led to its domination by shadow energies as a result of influences from other solar systems. In a deeper sense, you could say that Earth chose to go through this phase of ice cycles as part of its own perceived, evolutionary need.

So in time, human experience became more and more singular, in a similar manner to which a young child grows up within a family and needs to experience itself within its own sphere—it needs to generate its own life. However, this process got out of hand. What was thought to be happening for only a very short while has continued longer than maybe is necessary for that aspect of Earth's life which you are, as human beings, and also for many other aspects of Earth's life. The rule of fear has come to be seen and experienced as natural, which it is not. So the human spirit has indeed evolved through a number of forms, becoming less and less ape-like in appearance, and the more human beings have lost their instinctive awareness, the more their appearance has changed. For forms may change in a very rapid time, even within a lifetime.

Let us look at Neanderthal people first. They were here, indeed, long before your modern ancestors. They were here for many millennia—aeons—for they had evolved more from the earliest lines of human beings. In many ways they are more truly of the Earth, perhaps, than you are, in the sense that they represent in their shape that animal innocence. The sense of belonging to Earth is built into their physical form, such as the head and the face. Their instinct is expressed in their appearance.

Now, the controversy about the appearance of modern humans is likely to continue so long as science is blind to discoveries made through intuition and other sources such as channeling. For the appearance of modern humans was not only the result of biological adaptation to circumstances on Earth. What actually happened was the seeding of a new stereotype, if you like, a new form, from outside of this planet. The modern human shape did not evolve purely as a result of evolution on Earth. The absence of the pronounced brow—which is present in the configuration of the Neanderthal face and shows their alter major awareness—was seeded in order to enable human life to continue on Earth. For with the continuation of the ice cycle, and with the inability of the Neanderthal people to cope with this, human life could not have gone on as the shadow energies continued to squeeze life on Earth more tightly. What was required, in a sense, was a more evolved shape of the human. That alter major awareness, had it remained under the conditions of the ice, would have meant that the whole of humanity would have gone the way of the Neanderthals. Without that alter major awareness, people could cope with the ice.

In a sense, what we are talking about is modern humans not being completely, totally, of Earth's evolution, in the same way that Neanderthals were. Of course, the modern human form is to a large extent derived from the form which has evolved for so long on Earth. But in the earliest seeding of the Lemurian and Atlantean civilizations, there was a new input, a new impulse which was not quite so much of this Earth. This is why it is so important now for human beings to make that extra effort to link up again with Earth, as their earlier cousins had done so instinctively. Part of the aloofness and arrogance of modern humans could be understood as stemming from a kind of cellular memory—that the human form today is largely an amalgam, partly derived from the full lineage of human evolution upon Earth, and partly adapted, not so much by natural selection as by spiritual selection, as an input from a need to maintain human life on Earth. Hence the flat brow, the small nose, the creative intellect, the proliferation of language, all of which were apparent in those now-disappeared lines of the Atlantean and Lemurian civilizations. For in many ways they were apart from the mainstream of evolution. In particular, the Atlanteans became what you might call more unnatural in their activities, compared to, say, early 'Earth' people, including later on the Neanderthals, who were more truly of the Earth lineage. In a sense, they were more wholly human than modern humans— modern humans in the sense of humans traced back to the Atlantean and Lemurian seeding.

So the Neanderthal people, with that extended, instinctual awareness, could no longer maintain that extended awareness amidst the harshness of Earth's changing climate, shifting to and fro between ice and not ice. The Neanderthal people needed more stability, whereas the modern human was much more quick-witted and could adapt. The Neanderthals were not slow. They were simply so deeply attuned to the rhythms and cycles of the natural world that they could not shift themselves to be apart from that frozenness. If they had stayed on Earth, their spirits would indeed have frozen.

So what was their gift to modern human beings? For the two groups did live together for many millennia. They did not interbreed, for there was no biological attraction between them— between your ancestors and Neanderthal people. But there was a profound spiritual attraction between each other, and they did cohabit for a very long time in neighboring regions. While modern humans did, at one time, have the use of sound as part of their technology, the gift of the Neanderthals to the moderns—which laid down the roots of shamanism—was to breathe into the souls of your ancestors a sense of the wonder and awe of life on Earth, which those people could easily have lost. With their very adaptable minds, your ancestors quickly began to experience that intellectual consciousness which has become so dominant in your own culture today — the analytical view, but also the cut-offness from Earth.

Neanderthal shamans did not need to leave their bodies because they could see spirit and the spirits all around them. Theirs was a profoundly rich perception of life on Earth. It was not purely physical, for it was also what you might call astral, in the sense that they could see with their own eyes the forces which gave rise to physical manifestations. They could communicate directly with what you have come to know as 'the spirits.' But early on in the last ice age, after the eruption of that great volcano, and the darkness of years and years of night and ice, the Neanderthals knew that one day they would have to leave life on Earth. And as the great aeons of time passed, more and more of them did leave, and did not come back, certainly not as Neanderthal people. More and more came back as moderns.

So through reincarnation, Neanderthal consciousness was passed on to the modern human beings — not biologically, but spiritually. As the modern human mind contracted more and became more and more cut off from the natural world, it retained that capacity to extend awareness. It received that impulse from the Neanderthal memory of being able to communicate directly, and to experience that mystical participation with Earth's spirit.

The gift of Neanderthal people was that alter major awareness, that deep resonance of the past. That is what they cultivated, not only the deep resonance of the past, but also a profoundly elemental awareness of all the life forms around them — and that sense of danger. It was that sense of danger, which the alter major awareness brings, that caused them to withdraw from life. For the danger was upon them. It was impossible for them to contract — for those brows to shrink, for their noses to withdraw, for their profound reaching out to Earth to cease. While they were capable of what is called 'symbolic behaviour' — of making art — they were never driven to do so, like modern people became driven, compelled almost as a matter of survival to reach within. They could only reach out—for them inner was outer, and outer was inner. There was much less of that isolation of the prison and distinct barrier between inner and outer. So as they reincarnated into modern bodies, they were able to bring that knowledge, that deep, deep knowledge with them as an echo, as a vibration of the spirit. When the need arose for the 'modern' shaman to journey out of the body, that echo of their deep indigenous Neanderthal life and awareness went with them, so that they could reach out now from outside the body to the all-embracing awareness of Earth's spirit, as manifest in the astral worlds.

So, in a nutshell, it is Neanderthal awareness which brings with it the awareness of Earth's all-embracing spirit. It is a holistic awareness, whereas, left to their own devices, the consciousness of the moderns could have been purely manipulative. It would have lost all traces of the *participation mystique* which was the gift of your Neanderthal cousins."

Appendix 2 to Chapter 1
"Let your mind clear of all the daily preoccupations. You seek a clear perception of this ice-age saga. There have been many modes and forms of consciousness within the varying strands of humanity during its unfolding on Earth. In attempting to elucidate the evolution of your modern consciousness as a result of the ice-age conditions, which your ancestors experienced, you are indeed describing a certain pattern of contraction of consciousness, the compression of it within the human body—the analogy is appropriate. However, it is not the only reason for that great burst or explosion of creativity at that time. The creativity was not simply the result of the contraction and internalizing of consciousness from its previously more open and diffuse condition.

As you already know, a new, anatomically modern human being was seeded sometime before the onset of the last ice age, towards the end of the previous one, in order to be able to continue the human line through the unexpectedly long cycle of ice ages.

But even with the seeding of this particular kind of human being, which is what your ancestors were, there would have been a danger of them dying out with the ice, along with their Neanderthal cousins, if there had not been one further impulse specifically aimed towards them from sources beyond this planet, in particular, from the Pleiadean influence.

These people were impelled, and inspired, by energies which were from beyond this Earth, energies which were modified and attuned to suit a particular kind of more contracted, introverted consciousness, a more compressed consciousness. It was an impulse of joy, and celebration, and was very much responsible for the genius of the cave paintings. Those early shamans knew about this impulse, and they were not only attuning their consciousness to the world of the earthly spirits, but also towards the wider sphere beyond Earth. They were able to journey outside the ice and to allow their consciousness to be a bridge from those influences beyond Earth down into those caves."

NOTES

Introduction
1. Frank Waters, *Pumpkin Seed Point: Being With The Hopi* (Chicago, IL: Ohio University Press, 1969), p. 26. As found in Holger Kalweit, *Shamans, Healers and Medicine Men* (Boston & London: Shambala, 1992), p. 228.
2. See, for example, Roger Walsh, "Shamanic Cosmology: A Psychological Examination of the Shaman's Worldview," *ReVision*, vol. 13, no. 2, (Fall 1990), p. 87.

Chapter 1
1. Joseph Campbell, *Historical Atlas of World Mythology*, Vol. 1: *The Way of the Animal Powers* (London: Times Books, 1984), p. 47.
2. Ibid., p. 49.
3. Ibid., p. 25.
4. Ian Tattershall, "Once We Were Not Alone," *Scientific American*, (January 2000), p. 43.
5. Richard Rudgley, *Secrets of the Stone Age* (London: Century, 2000), p. 106.
6. Randall White, "Visual Thinking in the Ice Age," *Scientific American*, (July 1989), p. 77.
7. Ibid.
8. J.D. Lewis-Williams and T. A. Dowson, "The Signs Of All Times: Entopic Phenomena in Upper Paleolithic Art," *Current Anthropology*, vol. 29, no. 2, (April 1988), p. 213.
9. Joseph Campbell, *The Masks of God*, Vol. 1: *Primitive Mythology* (London: Penguin Books, 1976), pp. 305-306.
10. J.D. Lewis-Williams and T. A. Dowson, "The Signs Of All Times," p. 216.
11. Ibid., p. 215.
12. Vandiver, Pamela B., et al. "The Origins of Ceramic Technology at Dolní Vestonice, Czechoslovakia," *Science*, vol. 246 (Nov. 24, 1989), p.1007.

Chapter 2
1. Joseph Campbell, *Historical Atlas of World Mythology*, Vol. 1: *The Way of the Animal Powers* (London: Times Books, 1984), p. 58.
2. James Shreeve, *The Neandertal Enigma* (London: Penguin Books, 1997), p. 338.
3. Ian Tattershall, "Once We Were Not Alone," *Scientific American*, (January 2000), p. 43.
4. Peter Watson, "Mankind's golden stone of destiny," *The Sunday Times, News Review*, (6 February 2000), p. 7.
5. Paul G. Bahn, "Neanderthals emancipated," *Nature*, vol. 394, (20 August 1998), p. 721.
6. Joseph Campbell, *The Masks of God*. Vol. 1: *Primitive Mythology* (London: Penguin Books, 1976), p. 341.
7. Joseph Campbell, *Historical Atlas of World Mythology*, Vol. 1: *The Way of the Animal Powers*, p. 54.
8. Ralph S. Solecki, "Shanidar IV, a Neanderthal Flower Burial in Northern Iraq," *Science*, vol. 190 (November 28, 1975), p. 881.
9. Ibid.
10. Joseph Campbell, *Historical Atlas of World Mythology*, Vol. 1: *The Way of the Animal Powers*, p. 47.

Chapter 3
1. Fritjof Capra, *Uncommon Wisdom* (London: Fontana, 1989), p.152.
2. James Shreeve, *The Neandertal Enigma* (London: Penguin Books, 1997), p. 6.
3. Daniel E. Lieberman, "Sphenoid shortening and the evolution of modern cranial shape," *Nature*, vol. 393, (14 May 1998), p. 158.
4. Gildas, personal communication, channeled by Ruth White, London: June 6th 1991.
5. Ruth White, *Working With Your Chakras* (London: Piatkus, 1993) pp. 130-131.
6. Ibid., p. 131.

7. Ibid., p. 132.
8. Ibid.
9. Gildas, personal communication, June 6th 1991.
10. Ibid.
11. James Shreeve, *The Neandertal Enigma*, pp. 340-341.
12. Ibid., p. 341.
13. Ibid.
14. Ibid., p. 266.
15. Jean-Marie Chauvet, Eliette Brunel Deschamps, Christian Hillaire, *Chauvet Cave: The Discovery of the World's Oldest Paintings* (London: Thames & Hudson, 1996), p. 50.
16. Gildas, personal communication, June 6th 1991.

Chapter 4

1. Mircea Eliade, *Shamanism: Archaic Techniques Of Ecstasy* (New York: Arkana, 1989), p. 259.
2. Joan Halifax, *Shamanic Voices: A Survey of Visionary Narratives* (New York: Arkana, 1991), p. 103.
3. Robert E. Ryan, *The Strong Eye of Shamanism: A Journey Into The Caves Of Consciousness* (Rochester, VT: Inner Traditions, 1999), p. 115.
4. Jeanne Achterberg, "The Shaman: Master Healer in the Imaginary Realm," in Shirley Nicholson, comp. *Shamanism* (Wheaton, IL: Quest Books, The Theosophical Publishing House, 1987), p. 113.
5. Joan Halifax, "The Shaman's Initiation," *ReVision*, vol. 13, no. 2, (Fall 1990), p. 53.
6. Knud Rasmussen, *Intellectual Culture of the Iglulik Eskimos*, tr. William Worster. Report of the Fifth Thule Expedition, 1921-1924, vol. 7, no. 1, (Copenhagen: Glydendalske boghandel, 1930), p. 112. As found in Eliade, *Shamanism*, pp. 60-61.
7. Ibid., p. 113. As found in Eliade, *Shamanism*, p. 61.
8. Lorna Marshall, "The Medicine Dance of the !Kung Bushmen," *Africa*, vol. 39, no. 4, (1962), pp. 350-352.
9. David Lewis-Williams & Thomas Dowson, *Images of Power:*

Understanding Bushman Rock Art (Johannesburg: Southern Book Publishers, 1989), p. 70.
10. Richard Katz, *Boiling Energy: Community Healing among the Kalihari Kung* (Cambridge, MA: Harvard University Press, 1982), p.7. As found in Holger Kalweit, *Shamans, Healers and Medicine Men* (Boston & London: Shambala, 1992), p. 169.
11. Joseph Campbell, *Historical Atlas of World Mythology*, Vol. 1: *The Way of the Animal Powers* (London: Times Books, 1984), p. 95.
12. Lorna Marshall, "!Kung Bushman Religious Beliefs," *Africa*, vol. 32, no. 3, (1962), p. 251.
13. "Shamanic Practices in Tantric Buddhism: An Interview with Ngakpa Chögyam Rinpoche," *Shaman's Drum*, No. 20, (Summer 1990), p. 49.
14. James Cowan, *Mysteries of the Dream-Time* (Bridport, Dorset: Prism Press, 1989), p. 7.
15. Ibid., pp. 6-7.
16. Eliade, *Shamanism*.
17. Melinda Maxfield, "The Journey of the Drum," *ReVision*, vol. 16, no. 4, (Spring 1994), p. 158.
18. Carl Levett, *Crossings: A Transpersonal Approach* (Ridgefield, CT: Quiet Song, 1974). As found in Holger Kalweit, *Shamans, Healers and Medicine Men*, p. 55.
19. Eliade, *Shamanism*, p. 259.
20. Piers Vitebsky, *The Shaman* (Duncan Baird Publishers, 1995), p. 158.
21. Ibid.
22. Ibid., pp. 158-159.
23. Ibid., p. 17.
24. See Chapter 1, note 3.
25. Eliade, *Shamanism*, p. 99.
26. Joseph Campbell, *The Masks of God*, Vol. 1: *Primitive Mythology* (London: Penguin Books, 1976), p. 266.
27. Laurens van der Post, *The Heart of the Hunter* (London: Penguin Books, 1965), p. 188.
28. Ibid., p. 222.

Chapter 5
1. Timothy White, "Northwest Coast Medicine Teachings: An Interview with Johnny Moses," *Shaman's Drum*, No. 23, (Spring 1991), p. 40.
2. Mircea Eliade, *Shamanism, Archaic Techniques Of Ecstasy* (New York: Arkana, 1989), p. 508.
3. Timothy White, "Northwest Coast Medicine Teachings: An Interview with Johnny Moses," p. 40.
4. Ibid.
5. Ibid., pp. 40-41.
6. Joan Halifax, *Shamanic Voices: A Survey of Visionary Narratives* (New York: Arkana, 1979), pp. 73-74.
7. Timothy White, "Northwest Coast Medicine Teachings: An Interview with Johnny Moses," p. 41.
8. Holger Kalweit, *Shamans, Healers and Medicine Men* (Boston & London: Shambala, 1992), p. 224.
9. Eliade, *Shamanism*, p. 8.
10. James Cowan, *Mysteries of the Dream-Time* (Bridport, Dorset: Prism Press, 1989), p. 19.

Chapter 6
1. Laurens van der Post, *The Heart of the Hunter* (London: Penguin Books, 1965), p. 62.
2. Christina Grof & Stanislav Grof, MD, *The Stormy Search for the Self: Understanding and Living With Spiritual Emergency* (London: Mandala, 1991), p. 34.
3. Joan Halifax, "The Shaman's Initiation," *ReVision*, vol. 13, no. 2, (Fall 1990), p. 57.
4. Ibid.
5. Christina Grof & Stanislav Grof, *The Stormy Search for the Self*, p. 44.
6. Thomas Moore, ed., *A Blue Fire: The Essential James Hillman* (London: Routledge 1990), p. 98.
7. Ibid., p. 85.
8. H. Ostermann, ed., *The Alaskan Eskimos, as described in the Posthumous Notes of Dr. Knud Radmussen* (Copenhagen:

Nordisk Forlag, 1952), 97-99. As found in Joseph Campbell, *Historical Atlas Of World Mythology*, Vol. 1: *The Way Of The Animal Powers* (London: Times Books, 1984), p.169.
9. Ibid.

Chapter 7

1. David Spangler & William Irwin Thompson, *Reimagination of the World: A Critique of the New Age, Science, and Popular Culture* (Santa Fé, NM: Bear & Co, 1991), p. 25.
2. Spangler & Thompson, *Reimagination of the World*, p. 35.
3. Michael Vanney Adams, "The New Age—An Interview with Kathleen Raine," *Spring* (1982), p. 114.
4. Spangler & Thompson, *Reimagination of the World*, p. 35.
5. Ibid., p. 36.
6. Joan Halifax, "Shamanism, Mind and No-self" in *Shamanism*, compiled by Shirley Nicholson, (Wheaton, IL: Quest Books, The Theosophical Publishing House, 1987), p. 215.
7. Daniel Tujillo Rivas, "Navigating The Unknown: An Interview With Carlos Castaneda,"*Uno Mismo*, (February 1997). Reprinted in *Kindred Spirit*, Issue 39 (Summer 1997), p. 50.
8. Michael Harner, "What Is Shamanism?" Extract from the Newsletter of *The Foundation for Shamanic Studies*, (Winter 1990-91).
9. Daniel Tujillo Rivas, "Navigating The Unknown: An Interview With Carlos Castaneda," *Kindred Spirit*, p. 49.
10. Carlos Castaneda, *The Art of Dreaming* (London: The Aquarian Press, 1993), p. 42.
11. Ibid., p. 2.
12. Ibid.
13. Ibid.
14. Daniel Tujillo Rivas, "Navigating The Unknown: An Interview With Carlos Castaneda," *Kindred Spirit*, p. 50.
15. Thomas Moore, ed., *A Blue Fire: The Essential James Hillman* (London: Routledge 1990), p. 124.

16. Joan Halifax, "Shamanism, Mind and No-self" in *Shamanism*, compiled by Shirley Nicholson, pp. 221-222.
17. Jonathan Horwitz, "Return to Spirit: Shamanism and Responsibility," *The Journey Journal*, Vol. 2, No. 2 (Spring/Summer 1994), p. 10.
18. Gildas, channeled by Ruth White. Throughout this section, Gildas was answering a question, "About the American Indian rituals and their growing popularity," during a workshop at Glastonbury, Somerset, UK, (2nd August 1986).
19. Tad Mann, *Millennium Prophesies*, (Shaftesbury, Dorset: Element Books, 1992), p. 124.

Chapter 8
1. Laurens van der Post, *The Heart of the Hunter* (London: Penguin Books, 1965), p. 116.
2. Mika Amuru, "A Shaman's Statement," *The Journey Journal*, vol. 2, no. 2, (Spring/Summer 1994), p. 1.
3. Ibid., p.4.
4. Gildas, personal communication, channeled by Ruth White, London: (January 18th 1994).
5. Ibid.
6. Ibid.
7. "Shamanic Practices in Tantric Buddhism: An Interview with Ngakpa Chögyam Rinpoche," *Shaman's Drum*, No. 20, (Summer 1990), p. 46.
8. Ken Carey, *Starseed, The Third Millennium: Living In The Posthistoric World* (New York: HarperCollins, 1991), pp. 3-4.

REFERENCES

Achterberg, Jeanne. "The Shaman: Master Healer in the Imaginary Realm." In *Shamanism*, comp. Shirley Nicholson. Wheaton, IL: Quest Books, The Theosophical Publishing House, 1987.

Adams, Michael Vanney. "The New Age—An Interview with Kathleen Raine." *Spring*, 1982, pp. 113-132.

Amuru, Mika. "A Shaman's Statement." *The Journey Journal*, vol. 2, no. 2, Spring/Summer 1994, pp. 1 & 3-4.

Bahn, Paul. "Neanderthals emancipated." *Nature*, vol. 394, 20 August 1998, pp. 719-721.

Campbell, Joseph. *Historical Atlas of World Mythology*. Vol. 1: *The Way of the Animal Powers*. London: Times Books, 1984.

— —. *The Masks of God*. Vol. 1: *Primitive Mythology*. London: Penguin Books, 1976.

Capra, Fritjof. *Uncommon Wisdom*. London: Fontana, 1989.

Carey, Ken. *Starseed, The Third Millennium: Living in the Posthistoric World*. New York: HarperCollins Publishers, 1991.

Castaneda, Carlos. *The Art of Dreaming*. London: The Aquarian Press, 1993.

Chauvet, Jean-Marie, Eliette Deschamps, Christian Hillaire. *Chauvet Cave: The Discovery of the World's Oldest Paintings*. London: Thames & Hudson, 1996.

Cowan, James. *Mysteries of the Dream-Time*. Bridport, Dorset: Prism Press, 1989.

Eliade, Mircea. *Shamanism: Archaic techniques of ecstasy*. New York: Arkana, 1989.

Grof, Christina, and Stanislav Grof. *The Stormy Search for the Self: Understanding and Living With Spiritual Emergency*. London: Mandala, 1991.

Halifax, Joan. "Shamanism, Mind and No-self." In *Shamanism*, comp. Shirley Nicholson. Wheaton, IL: Quest Books, The Theosophical Publishing House, 1987.

— —. "The Shaman's Initiation." *ReVision*, vol. 13, no. 2, Fall 1990, pp. 53-58.

— —. *Shamanic Voices: A Survey of Visionary Narratives.* New York: Arkana, 1991.

Horwitz, Jonathan. "Return to Spirit: Shamanism and Responsibility." *The Journey Journal,* vol. 2, no. 2, Spring/Summer 1994, p. 10.

Kalweit, Holger. *Shamans, Healers and Medicine Men.* Boston & London: Shambhala, 1992.

Katz, Richard. *Boiling Energy: Community Healing among the Kalihari Kung.* Cambridge, MA: Harvard University Press, 1982.

Levett, Carl. *Crossings: A Transpersonal Approach.* Ridgefield, CT: Quiet Song, 1974.

Lewis-Williams, J. David, and Thomas A. Dowson. "The Signs of All Times: Entopic Phenomena in Upper Paleolithic Art." *Current Anthropology,* vol. 29, no. 2, April 1988, pp. 201-45.

— —. *Images of Power: Understanding Bushman Rock Art.* Johannesburg: Southern Book Publishers, 1989.

Lieberman, Daniel E. "Sphenoid shortening and the evolution of modern cranial shape." *Nature,* vol. 393, 14 May 1998, pp. 158-162.

Mann, A.T. *Millennium Prophesies.* Shaftesbury, Dorset: Element Books, 1992.

Marshall, Lorna. "!Kung Bushman Religious Beliefs." *Africa,* vol. 32, no. 3, 1962, pp. 221-252.

— —."The Medicine Dance of the !Kung Bushmen." *Africa,* vol. 39, no. 4, 1969, pp. 347-381.

Maxfield, Melinda. "The Journey of the Drum." *ReVision,* vol. 16, no. 4, Spring 1994, pp.157-163.

Moore, Thomas, ed. *A Blue Fire: The Essential James Hillman.* London: Routledge, 1990.

Nicholson, Shirley, comp. *Shamanism.* Wheaton, IL: Quest Books, The Theosophical Publishing House, 1987.

Ostermann, H., ed. *The Alaskan Eskimos, as described in the Posthumous Notes of Dr. Knud Rasmussen.* Report of the Fifth Thule Expedition, 1921-1924, vol. 10, no. 3. Copenhagen: Nordisk Forlag, 1952.

Rasmussen, Knud. *Intellectual Culture of the Iglulik Eskimos,* tr.

William Worster. Report of the Fifth Thule Expedition, 1921-1924, vol. 7, no.1. Copenhagen: Glydendalske boghandel, 1930.

Rivas, Daniel Trujillo. "Navigating The Unknown: An Interview with Carlos Castaneda." *Uno Mismo*, February 1997. Reprinted in *Kindred Spirit*, Issue 39, Summer 1997, pp. 47-50.

Rudgley, Richard. *Secrets of the Stone Age*. London: Century, 2000.

Ryan, Robert E. *The Strong Eye of Shamanism: A Journey into the Caves of Consciousness*. Rochester, VT: Inner Traditions, 1999.

"Shamanic Practices in Tantric Buddhism: An Interview with Ngakpa Chögyam Rinpoche." *Shaman's Drum*, No. 20, Summer 1990, pp. 44-52.

Shreeve, James. *The Neandertal Enigma*. London: Penguin Books, 1997.

Soleki, Ralph. "Shanidar IV, a Neanderthal Flower Burial in Northern Iraq." *Science*, vol. 190, November 28 1975, pp. 880-881.

Spangler, David, and William Irwin Thompson. *Reimagination of the World: A Critique of the New Age, Science, and Popular Culture*. Santa Fé, NM: Bear & Company, 1991.

Tattershall, Ian. "Once We Were Not Alone." *Scientific American*, January 2000, pp. 38-44.

van der Post, Laurens. *The Heart of the Hunter*. London: Penguin Books, 1976.

Vandiver, Pamela B., Olga Soffer, Bohuslav Klima, Jiri Svoboda. "The Origins of Ceramic Technology at Dolní Vestonice, Czechoslovakia." *Science*, vol. 246, November 24 1989, pp. 1002-1008.

Vitebsky, Piers. *The Shaman*. London: Duncan Baird Publishers, 1995.

Walsh, Roger. "Shamanic Cosmology: A Psychological Examination of the Shaman's Worldview." *ReVision*, vol. 13, no. 2, Fall 1990, pp. 86-100.

Waters, Frank. *Pumpkin Seed Point: Being with the Hopi*. Chicago, IL: Ohio University Press, 1969.

Watson, Peter. "Mankind's golden stone of destiny." *The Sunday Times, News Review*, 6 February 2000, p. 7.

White, Randall. "Visual Thinking in the Ice Age." *Scientific American*, July 1989, pp. 74-81.

White, Ruth. *Working With Your Chakras*. London: Piatkus, 1993.

White, Timothy. "Northwest Coast Medicine Teachings: An Interview with Johnny Moses." *Shaman's Drum*, No. 23, Spring 1991, pp. 36-43.